R. C. GREY

# ADVENTURES OF A DEEP-SEA ANGLER

*by* R.C. GREY

*with an Introduction by* ZANE GREY

THE DERRYDALE PRESS
Lanham and New York

THE DERRYDALE PRESS

Published in the United States of America
by The Derrydale Press
4720 Boston Way, Lanham, Maryland 20706

Distributed by NATIONAL BOOK NETWORK, INC.

Copyright © 1930, by R. C. GREY
First Derrydale paperback edition, 2002
Derrydale Blue Water Classics edition, 2002

Library of Congress Control Number: 2001097850
ISBN 1-56416-201-X (leatherbound : alk. paper)
ISBN 1-58667-079-4 (pbk. : alk. paper)

♾™ The paper used in this publication meets the minimum requirements of
American National Standard for Information Sciences—Permanence of
Paper for Printed Library Materials, ANSI/NISO Z39.48-1992.
Manufactured in the United States of America.

I GRATEFULLY DEDICATE THIS BOOK

TO

MY BROTHER—ZANE GREY

WHO MADE THESE ADVENTURES POSSIBLE

# CONTENTS

ꝮꝮꝮꝮꝮꝮꝮꝮꝮꝮꝮꝮꝮꝮꝮꝮꝮꝮꝮꝮꝮꝮꝮꝮꝮꝮꝮꝮꝮꝮꝮꝮꝮꝮꝮꝮꝮꝮꝮꝮꝮꝮꝮꝮ

# ILLUSTRATIONS

ᘯᘯᘯᘯᘯᘯᘯᘯᘯᘯᘯᘯᘯᘯᘯᘯᘯᘯᘯᘯᘯᘯᘯᘯᘯᘯᘯᘯᘯᘯᘯᘯᘯᘯᘯᘯᘯᘯᘯᘯᘯᘯᘯᘯᘯ

## ILLUSTRATIONS

ILLUSTRATIONS

[ xi ]

# ILLUSTRATIONS

## INTRODUCTION

*by*

Zane Grey

IT HAS always been a pet theory of mine that a man, especially a writer and a fisherman, should be judged by the nature of the effort he made and not by the result. That is the way I hope to be judged.

Several years ago I published an article about my early struggles. And now I want to tell something of my brother, R. C., about whom I write so much, who has gone the distance with me, the long uphill climb, the winding road, around every bend of which lay the unknown. Hard work is its own reward. What is truer than that through it one wins health and happiness?

Early in life, indeed when I was about half as big as the proverbial grasshopper, I took to fishing. My brother was then about a quarter of the size of a good lusty grasshopper. Strange to relate, he did not care about fishing. But in company with a coterie of wild youngsters he would chase chipmunks along a rail fence all day long. He would dig for rabbits and snakes, travel miles to find a new bumblebee nest, trap birds, and hunt squirrels. He became an expert squirrel hunter.

But little willow-bordered brooks and still eddying pools under a water-gate, and deep dark holes shadowed by a mossy bank, full of golden-flecked sunfish, and silver-sided little minnows, and yellow bewhiskered catfish, meant nothing in his young and otherwise very full life.

This childish limitation of my brother's was a grievous thing for me. I persisted in my determination to correct it. And by divers tricks and bribes and persuasions I eventually succeeded. Perhaps even then I had a premonition that I could never succeed as a fisherman and writer without the inspiration and companionship and encouragement of my brother.

Anyway, my haunts along Joe's Run and Licking Creek began to know the imprint of my brother's chubby bare feet. And the years grew apace.

I think I was about twelve when I took Rome on his first bass-fishing excursion. At that, his duty was merely to lag along and carry the bucket of live bait, at which he surely demurred.

At Bozemer's Rock I caught a nice bass, and lost the rest of my live bait, except the last, which I had on my hook. Then, so absorbed was I in fishing, I conceived the idea of sending Rome back alone to Joe's Run to catch some more live bait. It was monstrous. But I did it. His willingness, even eagerness, to go, would have been illuminating to me if I had been capable of thought at all. Here was a chance to do something himself, on his own hook!

Well, I can see him now, in memory's wonderful eye. He was a rugged urchin, round and freckled of face, with bright dark eyes and bright red hair, strong and slim, with his legs already giving promise of the fleetness that was to earn him fame on the baseball field as a young man.

He ran off, dangling the bucket, pole on his shoulder, whistling. As soon as he was out of sight my conscience began to voice itself. But though it clamored loudly, I did not yield to it until a sly bass slipped up and stole my last bait. Then I set out to find Rome, and the farther I went the more I realized my utter depravity. To send that kid off alone along a steep-banked run! And I remembered the day one of my playmates, Clive Lindsay, was drowned at the mouth of that place. I had seen the men wade ashore with his limp pale body. I ran so fast I soon reached the spot where Rome should have been.

He was not there. I found no sign of his bare feet in sandy path or on muddy slope. Frantically I ran along, yelling. And at last, to my joy and relief, I heard an answering shout.

Soon I stood above a high bank, gazing down as one spellbound. Rome was on his stomach, face down, sliding perilously nearer to the water. I yelled. His bare arms were outstretched, his hands gripped tight his fishing pole, which was almost all under water. He had a fish on and it was pulling him in.

Leaping down, I grasped his legs and pulled him up, in just about the nick of time. He clung to the wagging pole, and he did not say anything. Rome never was and is not now one to say very much. But he was surely lacing it into that fish, whatever it was. How tremendous the temptation to snatch the pole from him and land that fish myself! But I resisted it. However, I gave him as much and as good advice as I knew, which in my state of excitement probably was not very coherent, and when he at last had tired out the fish, a red-horse sucker as long as his arm, I scooped it out and got it up the bank to safety.

I was wild with excitement, and unutterably proud of him. But he did not think very much of that feat. He was cool about it, and called the fish a "son-of-a-gun."

"But, Rome," I expostulated, "did you mean to hang on to that pole?"

"You bet I did," he replied.

"Suppose I hadn't come?"

"Reckon he'd 'a' pulled me in, but be-gosh I'd hev stuck to that pole."

In time, when childhood years were long since passed,

we had two cottages on the Delaware River, at Lacka-
waxen, in the mountains of Pennsylvania. It was a wild
and beautiful region, abounding in game and fish. R. C.
here had ample opportunity to roam the hills with dog
and gun. He loved hunting. He took after our father,
who had always been a remarkable hunter, and nothing
of a fisherman.

But the mountain brooks were full of trout and the
river of bass. R. C. would not let me fish alone, and as
the years passed he learned the labor, the patience, the
endurance, the skill, and then the joy and beauty that
come from fishing inland waters.

One winter I went to Tampico, Mexico, and returned
raving of tarpon and other salt-water fish, all new and
strange to me. R. C. was always a sympathetic and willing listener. I filled his patient ears with my ravings.

Next I had my first tuna fishing off Seabright, New
Jersey. From that time, no doubt, dates my mental aber-
ration, so far as big fish are concerned.

Now R. C. had not a single drop of salt blood in his
veins. The idea of fishing in the sea was obnoxious, ridic-
ulous, and impossible for him. He said "No" with a
large capital. Nevertheless, it came to pass that one day
he went to Seabright with me and fished from one of
those dinky little Seabright dories, with two of the Nor-
wegian market fishermen.

It was a hot day. The sea was choppy. The Norwegians
anchored the dory and chummed for bluefish. The stench
of the decayed mossbunkers, which they used for chum,
beat that of the old slaughterhouse on Joe's Run, past
which as boys we used to hurry.

R. C. had never been on the sea. He did not know seasickness. But he was destined to learn. His face grew
green, and his agonies were terrific. He lay down in the

bottom of that dory in the hot sun and the stench for eight endless hours.

I was seasick, too. But I kept on fishing. My remorse and grief were not little, yet I could not give up and go in. But I think I felt at the time that R. C. was not so badly off.

We went again and again to Seabright, with similar results.

And after my several trips to Tampico, Mexico, in the winter seasons, I persuaded R. C. to go there, too.

But we never got any farther than Nassau, in the Bahamas. Yellow fever and revolution in Mexico shunted us off in the West Indies. We fished around Nassau, in the craziest kind of a launch imaginable, surely the first fishermen ever to troll a bait or spoon in those waters. We caught some small fish and raised some big ones. Two weeks of standing on our heads in a cockle-shell of a boat was about all we could abide.

We went across to Miami, and there heard about Long Key, where a few rich anglers from Palm Beach congregated to drag hand lines over the ocean. Another year at Long Key we had a wonderful time, and incidentally started what has become one of the finest fishing resorts and clubs that I know of.

The waters, though teeming with fish, were rough, and if I suffered, what did my brother endure? But I had a passion for the sea, at least for its beauty and mystery, and besides that, the most powerful of all incentives—the need of self-expression.

My many trips to the Southwest, most of which he has shared, except in the very beginning of my career, were no hardship for R. C. He loved to walk and ride and climb. A horse and a gun were enough for him. So I can pass over that phase of his achievement. It was a rocking boat and restless sea that took the starch out of him.

INTRODUCTION

Winters we fished in the Gulf Stream off the Florida Keys, and summers we devoted to Catalina and Clemente Islands, on the coast of California.

Ten years of this sort of thing had not made a sailor out of R. C. But the roll of the sea had long ceased to bother me. I had become inured to the heave of the waves, the glare of the sun, the whip of wind and spray.

R. C.'s first really great angling feat occurred about ten years ago, off Clemente Island, in the Pacific. He caught seven Marlin swordfish, besides fighting a giant broadbill swordfish, all in one day. He was on the rod from eight o'clock till six, that is to say, ten hours without a rest. This record has never even been equaled. Captain Mitchell, my associate in our New Zealand fishing venture, approached closest with six swordfish, and I came next with five.

It is quite useless to attempt to describe to laymen, and most fishermen, the labor and travail of such an experience. R. C. always claimed that my boatman and I "framed" the stunt and imposed it on him. He did not want to do it. He was never, or at least not for years afterward, proud of it. As a matter of fact, however, it just happened that the luck came his way early this great day, and after he had caught three swordfish, the third one a 328-pound Marlin that made sixty-three leaps, I laid aside my rod and coaxed him, until he absolutely would not take on another. That was some day. The ocean appeared alive with swordfish.

The years slipped by. They have a bad habit of doing that, especially for fishermen, to whom time is nothing. R. C. became the greatest Marlin expert of the day, and held that prestige until our sojourn in New Zealand.

No slight task was it to persuade him to try for a broadbill swordfish, *Xiphias gladius*, the true swashbuckler of the Seven Seas. He was five years in catching his first

[ xviii ]

broadbill, a 400-pound specimen, during which period he had every kind of experience with these terrific fish.

To hunt broadbills is the hardest kind of work. You roam the sea searching the water for the telltale sickle fins. Day after day, sometimes a week or two, we went without seeing one. Once we were seventeen days! The strain becomes terrible. The sea, the heat, the motion, the endless looking, the wait, are things few anglers can stand. Many and many a time R. C. has fallen on the seat to cover his eyes, and lie there till we got back to Avalon. Often we would run a hundred miles in a day. Seldom less than fifty, unless we hooked on, and by that I mean connected with a swordfish.

Prior to our first trip to New Zealand waters, R. C. was the only angler who had more than one 300-pound Marlin to his credit. He had five, 304, 314, 328, 334, and 354, the last of which was the world record until I beat it with a 450-pound fish.

The climax to R. C.'s nerve and endurance came on our second trip to the Antipodes. We struck a stormy season off the heavy coast of New Zealand, and in all we had forty-six rough days. When I say rough, I speak with moderation. Never in my life had I seen such seas. There were bright sunny days when the seas ran mountainous. We had come far; there was much to accomplish; and with Captain Mitchell and me indefatigable, R. C. would not rest. Often I importuned him to ease up, but he refused. And he grew thin and hard, with great white circles under his eyes. I really never suspected what that ordeal had cost him until we were back home.

"After New Zealand, our Catalina waters seemed like a millpond. I actually got some pleasure out of fishing," he said.

R. C. signalized this return by an angling achievement that I doubt can ever be beaten. During June and July,

1927, he caught seven broadbill swordfish, 291, 343, 357, 392, 435, 452, 588, the last of which beat my own so dearly won world record of 582 pounds. I might have begrudged it to any other angler, but not to R. C. He vowed he had greatness thrust upon him.

"You guys *will* make me go fishin'," he was wont to say to Captain Mitchell and me.

Of course, world records of the great game fish of the sea do not mean much to 99 per cent of people, but I wish to throw emphasis on the physical achievement. If you could combine the job of the sailor before the mast with the coal-digger picking on his knees, you might come somewhere near the hard work it takes to make the kind of sea angler I am writing about.

So much, then, for the test of patience, will, endurance, and muscle. Great as was R. C.'s expenditure of these, it was nothing to what it cost him to write.

Years ago I first broached the subject of R. C. writing of his experiences. He laughed at me. But at opportune times thereafter I had the temerity to persist. And then, some five years or more ago, we locked horns on the issue. The end of that argument, after the storm, ran somewhat like this.

"Sure you can write," I repeated, with that soft dropping persistence which wears away the stone.

"But I'm a rotten letter-writer," he replied, wearily. "You always said so."

"I never did."

"Bah! Blah!"

"But you can talk. Only last night I heard you tell those fellows about your scrap with those seven Marlin. They were absolutely absorbed."

"Well, that's different. Anybody can gab about a thing he's seen or done."

"It's not different. You can *write* as you talk. You're

[ xx ]

a keen observer. You have a good memory. Nothing escapes your eye. You are practical, contemplative, unexcitable. An expression of your experience on the sea would be valuable."

And so after a long time and in the end I won over R. C. to the idea of writing stories of his fishing adventures. At first it drove him nearly crazy, or perhaps that was because I kept everlastingly at him. When he quit taking notes and dropped back into the old quiet way, it certainly must have been tough to be jarred out of it.

Nature, apparently, had no more fashioned R. C. to express himself fluently than had it endowed him with my love of the sea. How thrilling always for me to try to write! I am still trying it. For R. C., how provocative of despair! But I saw clearly. He only thought he could not do it. He needed driving, encouragement, inspiration, and help. The first three I certainly fed to him. But I was always too wise and careful to correct his manuscript or write anything into it. That would have been fatal. But he did not lack encouraging helpers. And as to that, where is the author who has not been helped during the early agonizing stages of his struggle for expression? I have rendered assistance to many young writers, however, and I am now helping my small boy, Loren, who writes about "Specticular fights with barracudas," and vows he will become a naturalist.

To conclude, then, the things that count most with me are what a man *is* and how he *tries*. We are but finite. All of us are doomed to some failure. How long have I been shooting at the stars! The nature of a man's effort to do anything should decide much. Work is a blessing. The harder a thing is to accomplish, provided you stick, the better for you. Not only the connective tissue of muscle and bone is strengthened, developed, and perfected by laborious travail, but also the cells of the brain. That is evolution.

And so looking back on R. C.'s exploits, from the boyhood day when he hung on to the big red-horse sucker that was pulling him in, to the smashing and magnificent battle with his 588-pound swordfish, I feel that now I can be glad and proud that I made a fisherman and writer of him.

And reading over his stories, which have for me the singular and revivifying charm of provoking thrilling memories, aside from the pride I feel at having inspired them, I am happy and grateful for the vision given me, and sure in my conviction that his splendid efforts have earned their just reward.

╰╯╰╯╰╯╰╯╰╯╰╯╰╯╰╯╰╯╰╯╰╯╰╯╰╯╰╯╰╯╰╯╰╯╰╯╰╯╰╯╰╯╰╯╰╯

## TALE OF AN ANGLER

*by*

Millicent Smith

*To whom I owe thanks for helping me edit this book.*

NOW hark ye to my tragic tale—
 An Angler's life complete—
And learn the sore increasing trials
 With which this man did meet.

Fate cursed him from a little child
 With strange propensity
To snatch a rod with line and hook
 And roam where streams might be.

His mother with clairvoyant mind
 Foresaw his wild career
And Romer was the name she chose
 To call this offspring queer.

He had an elder brother, Zane,
 By fate decreed to write,
A sort of complex-natured cuss
 Who'd rather fish or fight.

With both the strain was in the blood
 But Zane's had salty smack.
On anything but lonely streams
 Young Romie turned his back.

And these he in his early youth
 Would fish both day and night;

[ xxiii ]

And tuna met by hundred scores
   A most unhappy fate.

He sweated, writhed and toiled and moiled,
   But Zane would not relent,
And made him cart a rod along
   No matter where they went.

Zane wrote by sun and candle-light
   And even lost his sleep
Recounting all that Rome had done
   To monsters of the deep.

Alas! Poor Rome—now Romer called—
   Had earned such rank through pain;
He never guessed his brother sought
   Some new uncharted main.

When Zane produced his stunning plans
   He had to acquiesce.
Off South Seas and New Zealand, too,
   He caught fish by the mess.

'Twas ever thus, year in, year out,
   With no relief in sight,
And Romer dreamed of brooks and streams
   What times he slept at night.

His haggard face was marked with grief,
   His suffering showed through;
His chest, once broad and hard and strong,
   Sank in a foot or two.

With shoulders bowed beneath the weight
   Of fame so dearly bought

And Rome would drag his boat astream
   And fish to suit his like.

The years sped by and all the world
   Knew Zane Grey's books by heart.
By fostering his brother's dreams
   Our Rome had done his part.

"If tales of fishes I would write,"
   Cried Zane, aglow with pride,
"Wherever I a-fishing go
   I'll need you by my side.

"For how can I attempt this thing,
   Without objective view?
The tales of other men's mistakes
   Must be supplied by you."

Rome trembled at these final words.
   "I can't escape!" he cried.
Though he put on a smiling front,
   His heart within him died.

And smiling to the seas he went
   An trolled the ocean wave;
But, oh, that cheerful face of his—
   The symbol of the brave!

He fished the blue Atlantic's coast
   And caught the sailfish there,
But seldom kept a meal intact,
   Which really was not fair.

Pacific swordfish ran amuck
   When he put out a bait,

[ xxv ]

TALE OF AN ANGLER

His brother Zane, close at his side,
  Would see he did it right.

"I'll make a mighty man of you,"
  The elder child would say,
"And give you fame in distant lands
  If you will do my way."

Unconsciously young Romie sighed,
  "I'd rather stay right here
And cast my hook out from a bank
  And use this simple gear."

His brother smiled a knowing smile.
  "Such folly cannot be.
Stir from this indolence of soul.
  You're doomed to follow me!"

And then the years toward manhood led.
  Our hero, now called Rome,
Deserted fair Ohio's banks
  To seek an Eastern home.

He settled by fair Delaware's side
  And thought he'd like to stay,
And when his brother spoke of seas
  He'd always run away.

But Zane was plotting as he wrote
  And piled the white sheets high.
(He'd knock upon the door of Fame
  Who still was rather shy.)

On off-days he would fish with Rome
  And stalk with bass and pike;
[ xxvi ]

## TALE OF AN ANGLER

He cursed aloud both day and night
    This thing that others sought.

Misfortune was attached to fame—
    He lost identity!
For Romie, Rome, and Romer once,
    Was Zane Grey's pal R. C.

Sometime upon a quiet bank
    Where trout meander near,
The worn-out carcass of R. C.
    Will find a lonely bier.

And o'er the turf at head and foot
    Two bamboo poles will wave,
And this pathetic elegy
    Will mark our hero's grave:

"Here lies R. C., grown old too soon,
    By fish trials sore opprest.
At some fair stream in angler's heaven
    May his sad soul find rest."

ADVENTURES OF
# A DEEP-SEA ANGLER

CHAPTER I

SAILFISHING THRILLS

IN JANUARY, 1911, Z. G. and I established ourselves in apartments in New York City in order to escape a severe winter in the mountains of Pennsylvania. But the mountain winter followed us down. That very month New York thermometers dropped as low as those of the higher altitudes from which we had fled, and the city was lashed and whitened by a severe blizzard.

As soon as the storm was over we emerged from our respective burrows. Snow lay deep on the streets and was banked along the sidewalks. Traffic was congested everywhere; exasperated drivers frowned from many a phalanx of automobiles held in abeyance by fallen horses, stalled trolley-cars and street-cleaning apparatus. People bundled in huge overcoats and warm furs, finding foot route the best route, forged against an icy wind or went scurrying with it, impatient to reach the shelter of places for which they were bound. We fell in with the others. We were frozen. Moreover, we were disgruntled because we had been cheated in our trade of climates. While moving along with the crowd we ran into an old friend, a dyed-in-the-wool New Yorker who thinks his home town is a perfect all-year resort, and when in no uncertain words we explained what we thought of conditions, he laughed and said: "Oh, I'm a regular Esquimau. You fellows better go to Florida again and thaw out."

Florida! He had said something pertinent. The damage was done. Plans grew, and February found us on the east coast of that Southern state comfortably located in Long Key's delightful fishing camp.  What a change from drab wintry New York with its bustle and confusion! All day the sun shone hot on the white coral shore and gentle breezes swayed the graceful fronds of palm trees, making sound like falling rain, and nights, softly cool, were full of delicate voices, the whispering rustle from the cocoanut groves, the lap of gentle waves on the shore, melody that lulled us to sleep. Each morning the ocean, in great blue movement beyond the opalescent reefs, beckoned us outward.

In the shoals at our very feet, where white coral sand and mats of brown seaweed showed through crystal-clear water, and out over the wide reefs which surround the key, fish life was prolific.

The yield of the reefs delighted us. The fish were so plentiful that excitement was sure and our fullest energies were tapped. Leaping fish, fast-running fish, and hard-plugging fish would risk most any lure; a strip of cut bait or a spoon overboard would produce immediate action. Savage barracuda would tear a small fish to pieces before we could get it to the boat, and big kingfish and large schools of amberjack would follow the boat for miles. A kingfish of forty pounds, a grouper of fifty pounds, or an amberjack of eighty pounds required from half an hour to an hour and a half of the hardest kind of work. I will never forgive Z. G. for encouraging me to make a specialty of grouper fishing. It cost me a day of pain and labor to discover his suggestion was a practical joke; after catching five grouper I had bleeding hands that ached. Never again! I lend a cautioning whisper to all grouper-angling aspirants.

These fish of the reefs, with dolphin, mackerel, and on the west coast the tarpon, were then the popular game species. Sad to relate, all, except the tarpon and dolphin, were being caught by the tons. Day after day, Z. G. and I watched big schooners roam the ocean with lookouts high on the masts, searching for schools of fish; every day we saw their crews cast their nets and load their holds with ton after ton of mackerel. As to the sportsmen, we noted with grim disapproval that most of their so-called angling was done with hand lines making possible the very ordinary day's catch (which in the end would be wasted) of six hundred pounds sum total. Others were blind to the inevitable result of such gluttonous killings. We saw, and our protests were misunderstood. Today Florida's southerly reefs, once the grounds of millions of these light-tackle sporting species, have only scant life.

In that early year of our experience at Long Key, sailfishing was in its infancy. Having a reef near at hand where fish could be hooked from daylight to dark, anglers gave little attention to the Gulf Stream, and so were unaware of its possibilities. Occasionally sailfish strayed to the reef, chanced to be hooked, and were sometimes landed. Anglers accorded them due admiration, but still continued to turn their backs to the dark rough waters of the stream, their natural habitat. Not so with the Grey brothers. Choosing days when the weather was most favorable, we rode the Gulf Stream from daylight to dark on single quest—the sailfish.

Often of an early morning, on the five-mile run from shore to stream we saw sailfish jumping far out. It was not unusual to see several in the air at once, leaping clear of the water, sky and horizon beneath them as they turned in somersault dives. Graceful and phenomenally agile, they made long plunges, raced over the ocean with sails widespread, or shot high above the waves, to drop like a huge sea bird foraging for food.

Whenever we saw them jumping this way, we speeded up the boat and tried to locate their area of action by keeping an eye on the patches of foam that closed over them. Then we trolled back and forth, covering the prob-

[3]

able distance they had meanwhile traveled. Many times we brought them up again; sometimes only one would rise, other times two or three would appear, and occasionally a large school would surprise us.

During our first few days' sailfishing we made many mistakes and hooked very few fish, but such ill luck we turned to profit by improving tactics and methods. One day, when we least expected action, two sailfish appeared behind our baits, zigzagging back and forth in lazy motion, undecided what to do. We watched in an agony of suspense. Suddenly Z. G. felt a gentle tap on his bait. He slacked off line. Then came another tap, this time stronger. On the fourth tap the fish took the bait and moved leisurely away. Quickly I reeled in my line to give my brother fair field, and meanwhile the fish speeded up and ran like a streak, breaking water just as Z. G. hooked him. He leaped in sidelong plunges and came right at us, circling the boat and making a heavy bag in the line. For a minute it looked as if he were off. But the line straightened again, the reel shrieked, and away the fish went. He made twelve frantic leaps in his effort to throw the hook. After that he settled down to fight it out. He fought stubbornly for thirty minutes, but gave in at last. He was exhausted when Z. G. pulled him to the boat, a beautiful well-formed specimen, about six feet long, with wonderful coloring of blue and silver and bronze.

On our way home that evening we saw kingfish jumping against a background of golden-red sunset, hundreds of them, large and small, leaping high in the air and flecking the rose glow with opalescent darts that crossed and recrossed. It made a beautiful picture. Always after that we arranged our return for the sunset hour when we could watch the kingfish play.

There came a day when we were actually surrounded

by sailfish. They were jumping everywhere. Several times our baits were charged simultaneously, but in our excitement we failed to hook the fish.

After I suffered several discouraging misses, a hungry fish made a frantic rush for my bait, grabbed it, jumped high in the air, soused down, and reared again, going over the water on his tail. I know he hooked himself. I made no motion. I was hanging to the rod, trying to recover from my amazement at his acrobatic performance. He was a marvel for speed. The reel screamed, the line smoked, and everything was confusion. Z. G. in his joy and enthusiasm was yelling impossible instructions, while the boatman stood aghast, bawling, "Look at him jump!"

My line was disappearing fast. I was staring grimly at the last few yards when the boatman, realizing in time that there was work for him to do, turned the boat toward the fish, which then seemed a mile away. Gradually I reeled in line. No sooner had I recovered almost all he had taken, than he started off again in long diving leaps, showing with each one his magnificent progress. I counted fourteen of these straightaway leaps.

Calm was restored on the boat and I settled down to serious work. The sailfish was out six hundred feet and going strong. We gained on him some, and after a while, for a second time I recovered most of my line. The fish, however, started a strange sort of play, running back and forth, dodging and turning; and then we noted a splashing in the water behind him. Before I had time to figure what was happening, the sailfish ran for the boat and under it, and following close came two sharks, one large, the other small.

I released all tension on the line and the sailfish lit out. Never had I experienced such a fast run! The reel shrieked. Fearfully I watched the line. A great bag

[ 5 ]

showed. He was coming back directly at us. I wound and wound until my hands ached. The sharks flirted through the water, trailing the fish. Z. G. yanked out a boat hook and at the same time yelled for a rifle. The large shark, of round yellow body and big blunt nose, was growing bolder.

"Good-by to my sailfish!" I yelled.

At that Z. G. opened with the rifle and some fast shooting followed. I saw a small hole in the head of the shark, and a thin stream of red colored the water. The shark turned over and slowly sank out of sight. Already his companion had disappeared.

This ended the battle. The sailfish was spent and came in easily, and we loaded him on the boat. I was the world's happiest man at that minute; I had landed my first sailfish after a worthy fight for him. Nothing could eclipse such a victory.

Consecutive winters found Z. G. and me fishing off the Florida coast. Each season our sailfishing methods improved. The sport was drawing more anglers all the time, and though other varieties had many champions, everyone declared the sailfish king. Surely as each new season came, reef fishing proved less attractive. No more of the boasted 600-pound catches! Indeed, some days there were scarcely any fish brought in. The schools were smaller and most of the fish were undersize. In time the fleet of mackerel schooners dwindled to a few boats. The ridiculously fat bags of unscrupulous anglers, and the steady draining by the market fishermen, were cleaning out the fish.

We had no patience whatever with the hand-line enthusiasts, but whenever we could we did our best to convert them. I recall one instance where we failed miserably until the person concerned suffered an object lesson which made our arguments conclusive. Said victim was a woman, a famous hand-line angler who visited Long Key in quest of new laurels, and wanted to try her luck on the Gulf Stream. Nothing we suggested could convince her that hand-line fishing was other than the greatest fishing in the world.

"You always catch small fry," I explained. "Out in the Gulf Stream the fish run large. Lightning sailfish, heavy amberjack, big fish that an angler can't stop even with long lines and good tackle. What would happen if you hooked one of those torpedoes on a hand line?"

She laughed me off. "Let me do my own worrying. I can hold them."

We happened to be on a fishing party one day in which our gay antagonist was included, and when she put her hand line over, again we protested. We received for our concern a faintly supercilious smile. As chanced to be the case, and fortunately for her, we thought, the fish were not biting. She sat patiently through the long hours, flinging a little fun at us now and then and challenging us to show her the great fish we talked about so much. The day advanced and the sun grew hotter, and she retreated to some shade at the back of the cockpit about twelve feet from the stern of the boat. Perhaps to relieve its strain for a minute, she bound her hand with a turn of the line. Had she been more amenable to suggestion, I would have warned her never to do that under any condition; instead I kept my peace. Odds having been against us, it seemed there was no danger of her getting a bite.

But the unexpected happened. She announced it with a sudden scream. Promptly she shot headlong out of her chair and struck the two-foot railing that circled the stern, which was the only thing that saved her from going overboard. We plunged after her and picked her up. She was white with fright. Her glove had been torn open and her hand was bleeding where the line had cut through and burned to the bone.

"Gosh! what a close call!" I ejaculated.

"Big amberjack," said Z. G. "I saw him, but I hadn't time to warn her."

We doctored the hurt hand and returned to camp. In a few days the unfortunate angler was around again, making plans for future fishing. She was game and confessed she had learned her lesson. "I guess I had better take your advice and go to rod fishing," she said. "Though I didn't see the monster that took my bait out there, and have only your brother's word for it that it wasn't a whale." Today she ranks high among expert anglers.

It was in 1923, twelve years after our first visit, that we particularly marked the changes in angling along the Florida Keys. We found there were no more hand lines and no more wasted fish. True, the fish were not so plentiful. Amberjack were much smaller, thirty pounds the average size, and kingfish were far below par. The reef fishing had changed to such an extent that it required patient trolling to bring any results; and tales of mackerel schooners to newcomers were questionable myths.

Each year more and more patrons flocked to the coast, men of distinction in the sportsmen's world, and many novices, for the sailfish had increased in fame and in number and were attracting anglers from everywhere. Women took up the game and won their laurels. The year 1923 was the most flourishing sailfish season ever known to the Keys.

That year we had a number of fine fishing days in February, but about the middle of the month we experienced a bad norther. We passed through a period of cold wintry days, fourteen in all, when idle, discontented anglers

SAILFISH LEAPING

The Beach at Long Key

grumbled against the fates. Northers are inevitable there during the winter months. While unpleasant and ruinous for fishing, they must be weathered if one wants to profit by the series of fine days which always succeed the storms.

When the February norther passed, the weather grew warm and the water calm and clear. Soon large schools of sailfish appeared, running south. During that time it was not an uncommon sight to see hundreds of fish in a single school, trailing near the surface and riding the swells with tails out of water. They traveled fast. To hook a fish, land him, and then find the school again and keep the pace, required quick work.

We went out on one of these promising days, inciting each other to do something worth while and show his mettle. En route to the Gulf Stream we trolled the reefs for barracuda. The water was furred by a gentle breeze, but clear, and there were striking cloud effects which occasionally cut the sunlight with shadows. Now and again, far off, we saw a sailfish jump. Z. G.'s cheers numbered their gyrations.

"Looks good today," he ejaculated. "Just counted nineteen jumps made by one sailfish. That's about a record for an unhooked fish. I hope you're feeling fit. No excuses tonight after I've beaten you."

"There won't be room for your couple of fish," I retorted. "The boat will be swamped with mine."

"We'll free everything but a gold-button fish," said Z. G., seriously.

Unable to resist such an opening, I returned, "That'll leave all the space to me."

In our early fishing years Z. G. seldom beat me at the game. Usually I had all the breaks, and he, knowing that, tried to stall my gaffs about his hard-luck angling.

We reached the Gulf Stream and headed for a jumping fish that disappeared on our approach. We trolled his

[9]

ground, and after a while he came up, a dark streak of bronze, behind Z. G.'s bait. He tapped the bait cautiously, and then, as the line slacked back from his touch, he took hold and ran. Z. G. made a pretty strike, but he jerked the bait away. He groaned and started to wind in, when—zip!—the fish took the bait again! How the old reel hummed!

"Better let him have it this time," I said, teasingly, "because I feel *I'm* going to hook one soon."

"Well, old boy, watch me!"

He struck one, two, three times. The light tackle bent double as the sailfish came out in a clean fine jump. I yelled—I never can help yelling at a time like that—and rapidly wound in my line. Then, having grabbed my camera, I clicked away, registering several good jumps. The fish turned on a leap and came toward us fast. The line was hopelessly slack.

"He's saying good-by!" I shouted.

But I was wrong. The fish was still there and going hard, jumping on his way. Eleven jumps in a straight line with sail widespread! A wonderful sight! It took Z. G. thirty minutes to bring him to the boat. When we freed him, a dazzling streak of purple shot through the water to disappear.

Our second encounter, which followed close on the other, was farther seaward, whither we were attracted by more sailfish sporting on the surface. We ran up on three of them. One snatched my bait on sight, but when I struck, much to my amazement, my line snapped in two.

Z. G. spoke up: "Hey! Go easy. These are not tuna. What do you want that nine-thread line to stand?"

I guess I was a little too strenuous. Anyway, I looked the line over and decided on another tackle. Before long I was ready for the fray again, this time rigged up with a twelve-thread line and a little heavier rod. Z. G. kept to his light tackle. He maintains that, for an expert, the sailfish is the greatest light-tackle fish that swims.

Sailfish seemed to rise round us from everywhere. The old desire to hurry came over me. Z. G. was alert, ready, anxious.

"Bad start for you, R. C.," he said. "Steady down and take more time. And let's see if we can't get some fine pictures today."

Two flying-fish, soaring toward us in frantic speed, just missed alighting on board; the wind had caught them and turned them in a graceful curve, and they sank on the top of a big swell. Their flight was significant. Big fish near! A second later Z. G. whistled, and I turned to see him strike. At the same moment a fish took my bait. I yanked it into him hard. Z. G. and I looked grimly at each other. Double headers usually spell disaster.

My brother's fish headed one way, mine another. I held mine as hard as I dared, and Z. G. let his go. They jumped and ran while we maneuvered the boat, running first toward one fish and then toward the other. We worked all kinds of stunts. When the lines crossed we changed places. I saw our fish in the air abreast of each other. Oh, what a chance for a picture! Farther out other fish jumped in play. Both fish continued to run and jump and leap and strain, but we finally tired them out, drew them nearer and nearer the boat, and eventually landed them.

We rebaited quickly and the excitement increased. Kingfish tore after our baits. There was a terrible vibrating jerk on my line and a powerful kingfish rose high out of water with the bait in his mouth and hooked himself as he soused back. He must have rushed the bait from the side. I held on wildly, but the hook pulled out.

Z. G. was laughing. "It certainly is coming to you today. Honestly, you looked scared."

[ 11 ]

"I was scared," I confessed. "He was a whopper, and he sure took me by surprise."

I studied the ocean. It was alive with jumping fish; the sailfish were still leaping sportively, and other fish were chasing schools of small mackerel and ballyhoo that fled before them. In no time we were involved in another double header, and a none too promising one, for the fish in their jumping crossed and twisted our lines. By careful manipulation we managed to untangle them, but it surely seemed hopeless at first. My fish tired quickly and came close. Yes, I thought he was mine, but the hook pulled out. I sat down meekly. My vaunted luck was not holding good.

Regarding with wonder how much strain a six-ounce rod and nine-thread line would stand, I stood by speechless as Z. G. fought. He played his fish with enviable skill, and finally won out. He tried to rile me with the protest: "I told you so! You were too anxious."

I kept my peace in faith that I would show him something pretty soon. A dull half hour passed, few fish, no action. Then suddenly fish appeared everywhere—great schools of sailfish. It seemed there were hundreds of them. They were all headed south and traveling fast, and each kept to a strikingly close formation. One large school was riding the waves with their tails far out of the water. I yelled like an Indian. Z. G. joined in. Here was the reward of vigilance, a sight we might never witness again; it made up for any number of slack days such as we had known.

The fish did not seem to mind us. We ran with them some time before we could head them off. We cut across the leaders. Then, with the wildest ferocity they rushed our baits, actually fighting each other for them. We both hooked on in a second.

The frantic motion of so many sailfish confused us. My

[ 12 ]

A Fine Specimen of Sailfish, 61 Pounds

ZANE GREY. NINE SAILFISH IN ONE DAY

fish made a jump clean over Z. G.'s line and tied us together. Disaster seemed imminent. However, the offending fish obligingly threw the hook, thus making the situation less ominous. I wound in rapidly while Z. G.'s fish ran away. My line was still wrapped around his, and as hard luck would have it a piece of bait still dangled from the hook. When the bait swung close to the boat, I pumped it up and down, trying to keep it above water, away from the hungry comers. Vain indeed was my effort. A fish jumped clear out of the water after it. I saw him snatch it, and another fish, angry at being beaten to some food, start full tilt after the more aggressive one. I let him run easily, not daring to hook him while my line was wrapped around my brother's.

While Z. G.'s fish was racing round over the ocean, with almost all the line out, a fighting devil of a sailfish tried to bite my line in two. I yelled to the boys so they would not miss seeing it. Four times he had the line in his mouth. Had there been strain on it he would have cut it.

My own sailfish milled in wide sweeps, evidently satisfied with the bait he had gotten. Fearfully I watched him. Z. G. could do nothing but let his fish run.

Time came when the strain on Z. G.'s line was too great; the line parted. Then I soaked it into my fish! The feel of the hook enraged him. He shot out of the water in lofty tumbles a dozen times. He turned upside down, walked on his tail, and, working up speed, shot through the water like a torpedo. We ran after him, circled back and forth and followed every lead. We counted twenty-three jumps. He was not going to take the water without a real fight! I was getting tired. I had my fill of thrills and excitement. Z. G., evidently satisfied, had put away his rod. "Go to it, R. C.," he ejaculated. "This is the largest sailfish you ever hooked."

[ 13 ]

The ebbing of my strength forced me to utmost care. The fish made no more jumps. He pulled stubbornly and steadily. We were both pretty tired when at last I dragged him in. He was my largest sailfish that season —seven feet six inches long, and weighed sixty-one pounds.

When we turned home, twilight was closing over the Gulf Stream, and through the soft gray shadow we could see the sailfish still jumping.

≋≋≋≋≋≋≋≋≋≋≋≋≋≋≋≋≋≋≋≋≋≋≋≋≋≋≋≋≋≋≋≋≋≋≋≋≋≋≋≋≋≋≋≋≋≋

## CHAPTER II

### TUNA FISHING YESTERDAY AND TODAY

ONE day, fresh from the joy of a tuna fight, I encountered Chappie, one of Avalon's most famous boatmen, and related to him a tale of the day's experience. I was courting a word of approval from this member of the old guard because his long years upon the waters, as both boatman and fisherman, gave his judgment of the prowess of rodcraft a well-earned precedence. But he offered me only a reprimand.

"Some folks forget that every today has its yesterday," he said, "particularly you sportsmen. Things come too easy now—that's the trouble. You profit by other people's achievements and never stop to think back to the old days when people had to buck things harder than you do. Why, with all the advantages you fellows have, the tuna game is child's play compared with what it used to be."

I had nothing more to say about fishing, nor had he. I immediately found the weather a most engaging topic of conversation.

Small wonder Chappie was scornful! I knew he had stories to tell which would make mine pale to insignificance. He belongs to that clan of boatmen who years ago made the tuna game famous around the world. One mentions his name when speaking of Michaelis, Mexican Joe, Enos, and other pioneer boatmen. Mexican Joe is gone, but the others are still here to tell of the thrilling days when men fought the tuna from a rowboat.

To fight tuna from a rowboat was a difficult and hazardous undertaking, yet it was done successfully. Success

[ 15 ]

was the result of tireless effort from daylight until dark, with now and again an unanticipated night upon the ocean. It meant long miles of rowing for the boatman who kept to his oars as conscientiously as a galley slave, and long hours of discomfort for the angler, who, doomed to a hard, uncomfortable seat, worked against time, the relentless ocean, and a fish. The angler's one convenience was his fishing belt, without which his attempts were futile.

The reels of the day were inferior, and drags of the present vom Hofe type were unknown. By bearing down upon a stick propped leverwise against the edge of his reel, an angler sometimes procured the effect of a drag. This and a thumb stall were the nearest approach to modern adaptations. It is not strange that men's hands bore the scars of fights.

In the early days of the Avalon Tuna Club, when an angler landed a tuna of a hundred pounds or more, it was customary for the club to present the boatman with a button. Though Chappie was one of the best boatmen at Avalon, a button fish seemed to elude his patrons. Friends of his wore the coveted prize, and their comments and assumed superiority rankled him. However, he bore his envy quietly, confident that every boatman has his day, and for three years nursed an unsatisfied ambition.

One season, a famous preacher visited Avalon and engaged Chappie for a few days' fishing. At the time Chappie was not advised of the calling and prominence of the angler, and when he did identify his man, since a freedom of speech few preachers condone was a deadly habit with him, his prospects seemed unutterably gloomy. Swear Chappie must, on slightest provocation, and fishing— nine times out of ten synonymous with misfortune—invited the widest exercise of his hectic repertoire. He set out the first day under premonition of disaster.

Throughout the morning all was well. Chappie leaned lustily on his oars while his companion trolled. But at noon, when some fish started surfacing, a tuna took the preacher's bait, hooked himself firmly, and made a rush for far horizons.

The preacher set to his fight valiantly, and Chappie made the oarlocks groan. After his first glimpse of the fish in the air he was rowing for a button. Minutes slipped into hours. It was Chappie's fight. In his joy he felt genuine affection for his companion, which waned only when the preacher gave evidence of fatigue and finally announced that he would have to give up. That was too much to bear. Give up! Whoever heard of a man-sized angler giving up? Throwing discretion to the winds, Chappie brought his forbidden vocabulary into full play, raving till the very timbers of the boat shivered. He defied the man to quit. In a frenzy of determination he grabbed part of a broken oar and stood on guard over the exhausted angler, promising violence if he dared give in. The poor fellow, in fear of his life, made a powerful effort, and in a surprisingly short time pulled the tuna to the boat. Immediately Chappie abandoned his weapon for a gaff, and while he was busy tugging the tuna aboard, the preacher collapsed.

Safely arrived in Avalon, Chappie was triumphant; the tuna weighed well over a hundred pounds. The day had come when he could swank along, wearing the long-sought button. The preacher, angry and still in a sadly dilapidated condition, went straightway to the Tuna Club, where he related his experience, sparing neither detail nor Chappie, whose waywardness he referred to Heaven for correction. But when the weight of his fish was announced, a rosier complexion covered events, and he beamingly ejaculated, "Good Lord! We got him all right, after all!"

Many long and exciting fights are on record at the club. One tells of a rowboat angler who spent an entire night working a tuna. It was afternoon when the man got hooked up, and when evening came with the fight still on, he refused, against the advice and pleadings of his friends, to abandon it. They brought him food, then kept within safe distance while he carried on. He stuck to his rod bravely, but after seventeen hours the fish escaped and the man was brought in exhausted.

Anglers of yesterday are credited with tuna catches as high as 160 pounds in weight. When one considers the risks these men ran, daring rough seas and the danger of capsizing of boats—for shipwrecked boatmen and anglers were often brought in by rescue parties—their accomplishments become proportionately greater. We of the present fishing clan at Avalon take off our hats to the members of Dr. Holder's time.

It was the introduction of power boats that gave new interest to the tuna game and increased its popularity. The first power boats were small, sixteen to eighteen feet, with engine power enough to carry them. The *Rival*, the *Pronto*, and the *Mallard* were boats of this type. When George Michaelis contributed the *Juanita* to the fleet, he stimulated others to vie with him for larger and more comfortable boats. (Michaelis' real triumph was the development of the revolving fishing chair which is universally used in the fishing launches of today.)

After a while the *Juanita* was eclipsed by Tad Gray's *Ramona*. Yet at the time everyone agreed that the *Ramona* was too large for fishing.

New boats appeared each year, showing increase in size, in engine power, in comforts and conveniences. Mr.

Catalina Tuna, 137 Pounds

156 AND 146 POUNDS

Conn, Mr. Doran, Mr. Brewster, and others, with their large and well-equipped boats, introduced the private ownership idea, and since then larger and more luxurious boats have been launched. In five years we saw Dr. Wiborn with the *Angler*, Dr. Alden with *Iris*, Mr. Jump with the *Ranger*, and now Mr. Spaulding with the *Goodwill*, Mr. Featherstone with the *Rainbow*, and my brother with the *Gladiator*.

The *Gladiator* is fifty-three feet long, with a twelve-foot beam, carries a Frisco Standard engine, has a gasoline capacity for a three weeks' supply, and is fitted with every contrivance that the builders and angling experience could suggest.

Catalina has given the development of the fishing launch great thought. For comfort, safety, and special equipment, I think the Catalina launch holds preëminence as the best all-round fishing craft in the world.

As the power boats were developed the fighting characteristics of the tuna were tested in new ways. Then there grew a difference of opinion among the anglers as to why some tuna are easy to land, and others of equal size are so hard to tire out. Many of our best rodmen, including Mr. Adams, Mr. Reed, and Mr. Bandini, have spent hours catching a tuna of 100 pounds and over, while at other times they have taken fish of a neighboring weight in less than ten minutes.

Mr. Adams worked three hours and forty-five minutes on a tuna of 145 pounds, yet he caught a smaller blue-button fish in eight minutes. It took Mr. Reed four hours and thirty minutes to land a 139-pound tuna. Place against this the records of Mr. Jump's six-minute fight and Mr. Bochen's seven-minute fight, both with heavy blue-button fish. I have watched Z. G. work anywhere from two to four hours on a heavy tuna. Again I have seen him land one of 120 pounds in five minutes.

[ 19 ]

What does this mean? Obviously that some tuna are harder to lick than others. But we anglers are concerned with the reasons, and on some of these reasons we are agreed. One is that the long slim male proves to be a harder fighter than the short heavy female. The other reasons may be applied to all fish, since they are derived from manner of hooking: the tuna hooked in the corner of the mouth is not hindered from closing his mouth and fighting hard; the tuna hooked in the throat and unable to close his mouth surrenders quickly.

It is the uncertainty, the ever newness, that puts the thrill into the tuna game. One never knows what is going to happen.

My first big thrill of the 1921 season came on one of those days of blue calm when the ocean seems to promise nothing and one trolls for several hours with no results. I was anxious for action and envied Z. G., who sat rod in hand, as blissfully unruffled as the sea itself. My mood was reaching the heights of resentfulness, when I suddenly became aware that Z. G. was intent upon something far off. Whatever it was he saw, no one else saw it. This is often the case, for he can see farther and better than anyone I know. Following his gaze, which led to the distant horizon, I too watched.

At once I anticipated Z. G.'s wild shout: "A school of tuna! Miles of them! Look, you duffer, away out there!"

Miles of them? Yes, it seemed at first there must be three or four miles of them. The great expanse of ruffled water moved steadily toward us—an army of tuna advancing for a charge. On they came, thousands in all, growing closer with each minute.

What a rare sight, and so unlike the schools idling on the surface! Only three times in five years have I seen a traveling school, and I am a faithful angler.

The tuna approached with astounding speed; as they tore through the water, they knocked helpless flying-fish right and left before them.

The unabatable onslaught brought to mind a remarkable episode of a former occasion when we ran into a school of tuna such as this. Z. G., out of thirteen strikes, none of which brought results, had seven fish broken from the single line and three from the double line, and in each case the break occurred before the fish had run far enough to cause any great strain.

A break from strain will occur on a single line, but will not cause a clean parting of the double line, so it seems reasonable to believe that in these instances the lines were cut by other fish. In a large school of hungry tuna several fish will spot the same bait and it is probable in the mad rush for possession that one becomes entangled in the line or perhaps deliberately cuts it. Playing for crevalle and snapper with a bright spoon in the clear water of the Gulf of Mexico, I have seen the other fish of a school take pell-mell after the one I had hooked, charge against him, then pass on to leave the bright spoon showing in the water as my fish disappeared with them.

Mindful of past experience, Captain Sid and I rigged up several baits and brought out some extra kites. If we were to get more than one fish, and if were to keep with this fast-moving school of tuna, there was call for speed and efficiency. The fulfillment of the fond hope for even one fish depended upon the size of those we happened to tackle.

The ocean was a seething caldron of bubbles, singing an endless song. Here, there, everywhere were flashes of bronze and blue. Z. G.'s rod was primed for the set-off of the fray. As we ran close, tuna rose from all directions and rushed the bait. Action was so sudden that the thrill of the moment was almost lost. A swift strike, then a tug of war was on! Short work, if possible, was the order of the hour; we wanted to keep pace with the hungry mass of fish.

Far out across the water larger fish cut and dove through the foam. Z. G. fought hard trying to engineer his fish so Captain Sid could work out toward the big fellows.

Time seemed lost in the rush of events. Almost before we realized it, Z. G. had a fish aboard and had cast again. Tuna were smashing the flying-fish all around us. To get a strike was only a matter of landing a bait on the surface of the water, for casting and striking were almost simultaneous.

I stood by, ready with fresh bait and a new kite. And Z. G. needed them! His second fish was brought to gaff faster than his first, and the excitement of the haul was still new when he hooked his third fish.

In angling, fish tactics have as much to do with the game as your own. You can't pump the fight out of a big tuna in two minutes, and you can't suggest what direction you would like him to take, which means you can't stay with your fish and the school, too. While Z. G. was working on his fourth fish, the school disappeared and the great wide wake behind them slowly spread and was lost.

In little more than an hour from the time we sighted it, the school of tuna had covered the two miles between us, and while we followed after, had passed on to a distance of three or four miles beyond our traveling boat.

Z. G. took his time on the last fish. There was no hope for another strike, and he was tired from the strenuous effort he had put into the other fights. Every one of his fish weighed well over 100 pounds.

When we returned to camp, we found that Lone Angler had got into the leaders of the school about ten miles

RECORD DAY'S CATCH OF BLUE FIN AT AVALON. AVERAGE 118 POUNDS

HOOKED ON

offshore and been cleaned out four times without stopping a fish. He said that 150 pounds was a fair estimate of the weight of any of the fish he saw. So, though we had had a wonderful day, we were at the wrong end of the school for the biggest fish.

There is a fickleness in tuna luck to which the angler must yield with grace. For instance, many anglers have never caught a 100-pound tuna, while others have taken a blue-button fish their first season. Then there is uncertainty about the tuna's appearance. Records show that sometimes as many as five years will elapse without any runs. Such irregularities make the game interesting for me.

It took me three years to catch a 100-pound tuna. As soon as I could say, "So that's that!" with all the pride of the wearer of a blue button, I raised my ambition to the 125-pound mark. Another three years slipped by, during which time I caught other blue-button fish running from 103 to 108½ pounds, but I never approached my new goal.

The 1921 season seemed as frugal in its promise as the past had been, and as the weeks flew by I became resigned to my fate.

You will remember I have already intimated that it is always the unexpected that happens to the tuna angler. So it was at the fag end of the season, when returning from a little scouting trip to Clemente Island where I had gone to see if any Marlin swordfish had arrived, I had a thrilling fight which I had not planned in my day's schedule.

Contrary to custom, we had left the Clemente shore when the day was well advanced. Usually boatmen arrange to leave early in the morning to avoid the rough water that courses through the channel in the afternoon.

[ 23 ]

But I felt no concern for our safety aboard the *Gladiator*. She had proved her worth in bad water, and though I have never enjoyed sailing a heavy sea, I do not mind it on the *Gladiator* as I do on smaller boats.

I knew many a large tuna had been taken by anglers while crossing from Clemente to Catalina, still it was more for the want of something to do than from the hope of a catch that I put out a kite. We headed straight for Seal Rocks, and as the wind was in the right direction, we did not vary our course any.

I watched the shores of Clemente fade in the fog while the waves grew larger and the wind stronger. Sid, in the hope of sighting tuna, sat on top and braved the cold wind till it drove him down. Neither Sid nor I love the ocean too well, and whenever the afternoon wind commenced to blow and the water showed white, a straight line for home was usually our course, unless, as sometimes happened, we were hooked to a fish. So when Sid swung down to join me, he voiced his disappointment.

"Bad sea," he said. "Getting pretty rough for fishing, R. C. Let's hook her up."

"I agree with you on the weather," I returned, "but I have a hunch about as lively as this sea that something is going to happen."

"You're right there," Sid growled, "and it's going to happen to both of us if this keeps up."

Without attempting to belittle the seriousness of his expectations, I tried to convince Sid of the seriousness of mine.

"I tell you this is tuna water, Captain, and I'm doomed for a strike!"

"Mmm!" he assented, disinterestedly.

I suppose there are plenty of fishermen such as I—and one born every minute—who would not admit that the sea was too rough for fishing, but I was right that it was

great tuna water, for so it turned out to be. Yet I say—
deliver me from any more of it!

Just when I was beginning to weaken under Sid's
scorn, near by, out of the high waves, burst a bunch of
tuna literally tearing the water to pieces. They were after
my bait. Instantly I struck and struck hard, and as I stood
all aquiver from the suddenness of it, I felt the first run
of a powerful fish. Sid turned the boat head into the sea.
The spray washed over me, and then I realized how fool-
ish I had been to continue trolling. But the thrill of the
fight was on me. It was as impossible for me to cut the
line as it was for the sea to be calm in the teeth of
the wind.

Remarkable to relate, throughout the long precipitant
run nothing broke. The defiant tune of the reel thrilled
me. I watched the line go—700 feet, perhaps—now 800;
and by the time 1,000 feet of my 1,500 slipped off, I grew
dizzy.

We were after the fish before the run ended, which
probably saved the line. Past experience in a game always helps. I gave the fish my full strength. I realized I
could not last long in that sea. I knew it must be a short
fight or none. Visions of a three- or four-hour struggle
flashed upon me and I actually trembled at the thought.

There is little to tell about the battle. Sid says it was
a great exhibition of determined play and that at times
he would not have given much for my chance. All I can
recall is pulling as I had never pulled before, and wondering why the rod or line did not break. I remember the
infernal roll of the boat and the deadening chill as each
succeeding wave broke over me, and figuring how long it
would be before the fish, pulling the rod from my numb
hands, would disappear, tackle and all.

When I saw Sid reach for the gaff, I marveled. I had
been strangely insensible to the progress of the fight.

Figured by time, it seemed only a few minutes since I had hooked the fish; figured by the countless aches and pains that pricked me and by the sudden assertion of complete fatigue, it seemed an eternity.

Sid leaned over the side of the boat and made a powerful lunge. I still could not believe my eyes. Through the scattering spray I saw his big shoulders move. Then he yelled for another gaff. I tried to reach out of the chair, but my legs would not hold me. I sank down, waiting for a resurge of strength.

There stood Sid, half out of the boat, still hanging on. His shoulders sagged with the rush of the fish.

"Give me just a minute," I panted. "I'm all in!"

The motion of the boat was maddening. As each wave hit her, I expected to see Sid go overboard. He had that horrible pallor of seasickness.

Another few seconds and I had reached for the gaff, and with feverish effort I plunged it into the fish. Sid and I lifted and strained together, staggering helplessly in our effort to get a sure footing. Then a big wave swung the fish upward and we pulled him aboard.

My big tuna for which I had been fishing three years lay gasping at my feet! A smile lit up the gray-greenness of Sid's face.

"You picked a bad day, but you sure picked a good fish," he said. Then pointing to the clock, "One hour and forty-four minutes!"

"Never again!" was my emphatic comment. "I've caught all the big tuna I want."

At the moment I meant what I said, but later when I found my fish weighed 137 pounds, I knew the day would come when I would aim to surpass even that.

Tuna fighting yesterday and tuna fighting today! The angler of yesterday was braver and more daring than the angler of today, and to him go the greenest laurels. Still it seems to me that he missed so much! No chance to pick four fish while almost abreast of a traveling school of tuna. No chance for a winning fight in the heavy seas of a mid-channel with a sure safe-home to Catalina's shores!

The sportsmen of this generation will pass on, become like others, anglers of yesterday, but through all time lovers of the tune of the reel, seeking a place "where sweet content her harbor holds," will turn to Catalina, that peaceful haunt whose fame has traveled round the world.

CHAPTER III

BIG TUNA OF THE ATLANTIC

MANY years ago, at Seabright, New Jersey, my
brother and I saw our first big North Atlantic
tuna. There the market fishermen and anglers call them
horse mackerel, but they are identically the same fish as
the tuna of California and the Mediterranean, and the
*tunny* of the British Isles, only they are the giants of their
world-famed family.

In California, the 100-pound blue-button tuna, such
as Chappie craved, is a weight above the average; in the
European waters a 500-pound catch seems staggering;
but on the North Atlantic coast 1,000-pound tuna are
common size, a 1,500-pounder not unusual, and the commercial record stands 1810.

We visited Seabright because we wanted a sportsman's
go at these fish, not the big ones, to be sure, but at some
of the juniors of the species. Our idea seemed prepos-
terous to the market fishermen.

"You don't mean you want to try and catch horse
mackerel with a rod and line?" one old fellow protested.
"Why, boys, you're plumb crazy! It can't be done. Why,
you couldn't even scratch the little ones. As for them big
busters, they grab bluefish away from me and break my
heavy lines fast as I put 'em out. It's a bad day for me
when they come into my slick after the bluefish."

We plied the man with questions and were advised
among other things of the meaning of the term "slick,"
as used locally. This slick was a long greasy trail of fish
oil come from the finely ground menhaden which the
market men spread around their boats to attract the blue-

fish. We were exceedingly interested. We intended to learn more about slicks and menhaden chum.

Much as the old man disapproved of us, he was finally induced to take us fishing, and we set out with him one morning, long before daylight, in a small boat, shot the turbulent surf and hied off twenty miles or more to sea.

With sunrise the ocean turned smooth and the large slick we had spread around the drifting boat looked like an ugly stain on a luminous crystal. Patiently we awaited the arrival of the bluefish. A sea gull soared above us and occasionally dipped down to pick up a small piece of menhaden, and once a porpoise fooled us into false anticipation by breaking the water near by. It was too early to expect tuna. The bluefish had to arrive before we stood the slightest chance at our game.

Z. G. was the first to see the bluefish come on. For a while only a few showed. As others appeared I ground out chum furiously to keep them interested and to draw more, and it was not long till they schooled around us by the hundreds, then the thousands, and so close they might well have been eating out of our hands. They streaked the green water with color and action. Z. G. and our boatman hand-lined bluefish fast as they could go, and I had a try at it, too. The way the old fellow piled them aboard was magnificent to behold.

Shouts from Z. G., amazing oaths from the boatman, and resounding and multiplying splashes from behind us announced the arrival of the tuna. Sure enough, swarming in upon the stampeding bluefish and driving them to precipitant flight were great barrel-bodied monsters whose size and speed rendered me speechless with wonder. Voraciously they gathered in bluefish and chum at the same mouthful. They smashed the water everywhere. Havoc increased as their numbers increased.

One powerful fish cleared the water near us, made a

turn in the air, and dove head first into the school of fleeing bait. Years afterward, when fishing in the Pacific, I time and again saw smaller tuna employ the same antics and came to the conclusion it was a means of feeding common to them all.

We were soon a demoralized lot. Z. G. threw a bait into the seething water. Instantly it was snatched with a violence so great that he almost went overboard trying to save his rod. On the tuna's first terrific rush the line parted. I dropped a bait over, had a strike, and the next minute bemoaned the new leader I had lost. Again and again we tried. It was useless. Rods snapped under the strain of the first onslaught, and lines parted as easily as cotton thread. Then and there began our education on the subject of fishing-lines.

With characteristic stubbornness we persisted; we could not say die till the bluefish had all departed, with the tuna in their wake and nary a fin cut the water near us.

We were completely routed, dazed, and forlorn. The magnitude of the adventure, its thrill and strain, left us weak. The boatman treated us like small children who had been too wise and over-ambitious and peremptorily assumed we were done with our nonsense. For the time we were—yes. But not forever. Perhaps it was because that evening we saw, close view, a 1,000-pound tuna which had been caught in a net and hauled ashore. It was a stunning sight. All Z. G. said was, "We'll get one some day, Red."

Memory of our day of tuna fishing off Seabright stayed with us always. In years that followed we devoted most of our time to Florida and the west coast, and in Catalina waters started a fight for modest tuna laurels.

THE STRIKE

THE GREAT HORSE MACKEREL

We fished faithfully, bearing in mind that some time we would try our luck with the big fish.

Z. G. and I never underestimated the strength and fighting qualities of the tuna of the Pacific. Many were the days, weeks, even months we devoted to pursuit of them, and many a thrilling and hard battle they gave us. Outstanding with such experiences as I have already related was a day when several schools of tuna bore down on us at once and we hooked eleven and landed six, the greatest one-day catch of them ever brought in to Avalon. The smallest weighed 114 pounds and the largest 130.

Bit by bit we improved our methods and developed rods, reels, and lines that would make pursuit of mammoth deep-sea fish a fair sporting game.

On one of our visits to New York we had the good fortune to meet Captain Laurence D. Mitchell of Nova Scotia—now the beloved "Cappy" of our outfit—an expert trout and salmon fisherman who at that time held the record for the largest tuna ever taken on rod and line. We had been primed for such an encounter on reading, a few days before, a magazine article which showed photographs of giant tuna caught by market fishermen at Cape Breton Island. All we needed was to have Captain Mitchell, with his delightful and infectious enthusiasm, tell us about his 710-pound record catch. Immediately Z. G. was sold on the idea of a trip to Nova Scotia.

In discussing ways and means Captain Mitchell said all Nova Scotia tuna angling was done from eighteen-foot rowboats manned by two sturdy oarsmen. He described long battles and hair-raising escapes and countless failures out of hundreds of attempts, all made by the same few sportsmen. Not a half dozen fish had been taken, and those by a Canadian angler named Ross, the English angler, Mitchell-Henry, and Captain Mitchell. This Z. G. laid to primitive methods and suggested the introduction of motor-boats. They had, it seemed, been tried and abandoned as useless in that particular game. Our experience with them for swordfish and Pacific tuna fishing led us to object to such a judgment on them. Z. G. was firm in his conviction that fishing from a launch was the better method.

Since the Nova Scotia expedition could not materialize for more than a year, there was ample time to prepare equipment. Z. G. had two special rowboats built after Captain Mitchell's design, and a launch after plans of his own. The launch, of a type to draw very little water, was to be small and flat bottomed, and equipped with two engines on which she could travel sixteen knots an hour.

There were no reels on the market adequate for such fishing, so Z. G. arranged with J. A. Coxe, the Los Angeles reel expert, to make some that would hold eighteen hundred feet of thirty-nine-thread line. This necessitated preparation of special machinery, for which reason it took a year to build the first reel of the new design. Our rods were made by Murphy of the best hickory he could find, and with those and better and stronger Swastika lines, we were ready for fair fight with the great Atlantic tuna.

The date when we were to meet Captain Mitchell in the town of Liverpool, Nova Scotia, had been set for early July, and that year of mightier quests we quit Catalina fishing in June without reluctance. Our two boatmen, Captain Sid Boestler and Captain Bob King, one of Z. G.'s Florida men, went on ahead to prepare for our arrival and try out our new launch which had been made in the south under King's supervision.

After a hot trip across the continent and a foggy crossing from Boston to Yarmouth which made us fearful about local weather conditions, we came to the woods and green pastures of the land of Evangeline. Glimpses of lakes and streams warped me out of my orbit so completely I could have dropped off the back of the train and stolen away for a try at trout. But when the train ran along the sea, giving us a splendid view of the rock-ribbed coast, I thought of that day off Seabright, of the giant tuna on the beach and Z. G.'s avowal, "We'll get one some day, Red."

At Liverpool we were met by Captain Mitchell and a delegation of citizens who gave us hearty welcome and their kind wishes for our success. Everything was ready for us but the tuna which had not yet come in. However, news that the herring fishing was improving daily took the edge off our disappointment, for when herring run well tuna are not very far behind.

On all sides we met skeptical comment about our hope of catching tuna from a launch. The market men were inclined to take it as a joke. Z. G. and I felt secure. We were there to try both skiffs and motor-boat, and we knew if a tuna would take a herring from a skiff he would also take it from a launch.

Our first few days of scouting along the shore opened our eyes to the beauty of Nova Scotia and gave us an intimate feeling for the great wide bays where yearly the giant fish came to feed. Off at dawn each morning, we ran out to the herring nets on chance of finding a stray tuna in search of a cheap meal. In season the tuna are a nuisance and expense to the market fishermen. They mill around the nets while they are being lifted, to snatch up what fish slip through, and often cut into them with their tails in effort to knock the herring loose. We saw herring by the millions, but no tuna, and had to reconcile ourselves to the dull hours that must follow.

We went from net to net, and here and there had chats

with the fishermen. From them I learned that schools of herring five to twenty miles square ride the waters off Nova Scotia. How do these fish happen to be so prolific? It staggers me. They come and ever come despite destruction by man and their enemies in sea and air. To estimate the total number of herring destroyed annually would be impossible. Ten or twelve billion are caught each year by market fishermen, yet that is figured as only five per cent of the total loss. The rest is laid to feeding fish and birds, and it mounts to many hundreds of billions.

For years ichthyologists have been trying to determine the route the herring follow in their migration, but to date they have made little advance in their study. These are the only facts available: when the herring leave Nova Scotia, they next are seen off the coast of Ireland, and from there they disappear into the sea to go a solitary way far from the tracks of man.

The first day, after the herring nets had been lifted, we fished awhile for halibut and pollock. The halibut grow to great size; often there are catches of 200- and 300-pound fish. The record halibut, caught off the coast of Massachusetts, weighed 625 pounds. The pollock is a game fish and so savage a fighter that one will keep an angler busy for some time. Schools of them break into the ranks of young cod and snatch up those delectable fish with a voraciousness that would make a Bostonian groan.

Reports of a tuna sighted sent us on chase to Port Mouton, a small fishing village. But we combed the sea there in vain.

Wherever we happened to be we ran into some town each afternoon late, to make a call at the fish markets and piers where coastwise boats unloaded their catches, and begged crumbs of news about tuna. Fishing schooners, returning from the Banks, brought in great masses of hali-

The Author with His 639-pound Tuna

ZANE GREY WITH WORLD-RECORD TUNA, 758 POUNDS

but and some harpooned swordfish, but neither they nor the many herring boats had any pertinent word for us.

The best of a week went by, and still we were no nearer our goal. We had scouted the coast for miles and knew every fisherman on the beat, and any one of them would have welcomed a torn net if thereby he could have been the bearer of tuna tidings. We heard indirectly of a few that had been seen distantly, but no catches were reported. It was a trying time for us; nevertheless, we kept our interest alive. Many a fishing trip that at first steeped us in disappointment had ended in a blaze of glory.

Captain Mitchell, who had helped us in every possible way, was less patient than we, because he had led us to expect so much and his promises were deferred. I wondered about the advisability of keeping Liverpool as our base, and the very day after I brought the question to Z. G.'s attention word came in by telephone that three tuna had been harpooned at Jordan Bay, forty miles south.

All other places were too small to hold us then. We fitted out another boat, one with sleeping accommodations and a small stove for light cooking. We were pressed for space and our commissariat was nothing to brag about, but we had reached the point where comfort was not considered. Anything to get the tuna. It had taken long planning to make this trip possible and we would let nothing upset our chances of success.

At Jordan Bay we were brought alongside an old wharf where we were free to tie up and land what fish we might catch and raise a tripod for them. A fog which had hung over the coast for two days lifted several hours after our arrival at the bay and out of the pall came the low hills and the shore line and the gray-blue sea.

That afternoon, grimly determined to have some kind of action, we resorted to the methods of the Seabright fishermen, and bought a barrel of herring to grind into chum. We ran out to the middle of the bay, Z. G. aboard one boat, Captain Mitchell and I aboard the other, and there we hove up alongside and drifted. We made a slick that would have been irresistible to a Jersey tuna, then settled down to watchful waiting. Detecting a commotion on the water about half a mile seaward, I concentrated my attention on it and presently caught sight of large fins and tails flirting on the surface. First I thought of porpoise and blackfish. In another minute I yelled, "Tuna! Tuna!" and heard the others take up the cry.

There were three of them, round long fellows. They passed through the slick without evincing the slightest interest. At once we pulled up anchor and ran ahead of them to put over some bait. We circled to a good position and watched their approach. They charged through the water, leaving a wide wake on their trail. When they got within a hundred yards of us Bob threw a herring out to them. It sank part way, but not before one of the tuna saw it. There was a savage rush, then a black back and a cloud of spray closed over the place where the herring had disappeared. Z. G. worked like fury to get his bait to him, but the tuna was done with second-hand fish. Later we ran upon another school, and after that a third, all luckless, for what few passes they made at the baits we threw over were half-hearted. We were not going to find Nova Scotia tuna amenable to that method.

We discounted our failures and closed the day with rejoicing. Tuna were working in the bay; they were with us at last. Captain Mitchell was indeed happy. He assured us that early the next morning, round about the herring nets, we would have strikes aplenty.

When we reached shore the market fishermen told us they had a tuna in their weir and had delayed taking him out so we could see how it was done. Glad of the chance to learn something new, we piled into the skiffs and rowed out to join them.

The weir was a clever trap made of upright saplings which bordered a mazelike passage and a large inclosure at the passage end. Fish that had come up the maze milled round in the inclosure, too confounded to find their way out. With them swam a large tuna. We hung on to the saplings and peered through. The market fishermen had come around into the inclosure in two skiffs. From the skiffs which moved in opposite directions, skirting the saplings, they spread a deep net, and as soon as they encircled the tuna with it they swiftly closed in on him.

When the tuna awoke to his predicament he grew frantic with terror and put up a spectacular fight, threshing the water, the weir, and the net with quivering blows, drenching us all and nearly swamping the fishermen. One of the men drew a large mattock and whacked away at the tuna's head. It took a dozen powerful blows to subdue the poor creature, and it was sickening to see him battered so.

On shore, fresh from the water, the fish shone in the full glory of his coloring, blue and silver, with faint side streaks of rose. His size to us was tremendous. When we were told he was a small one and would not weigh more than 500 pounds, we had nothing more to say. I think we were wondering what a big one would look like. I said then and there that if I had the good fortune to catch a 500-pounder I would be the happiest fisherman on earth.

The next morning, before daylight, in a heavy fog through which came the chilling moan of horns and buoy bells, we ran out five miles to the entrance of the bay where our stanch allies, the market men, were accustomed to set their herring nets. Already their boats were partly loaded. They said several tuna had been bumping the nets and advised us to get busy. We bought a barrel of herring from them, tied our launch to one of the net buoys, and planned our course of action.

Z. G. alone put out a bait. The rest of us were to toss occasional herring overboard and scan the water for fins. We all labored under suppressed excitement. Z. G. could hardly sit still. The thought of what might happen if we hooked a fish in that tangle of nets kept us nervously alert.

After a half hour at that post, with no action, we changed to another buoy. The fishermen worked on, hauling the nets with their tons of herring. We were almost agreed that the tuna had quit us, when suddenly one of the fishermen stationed far out shouted: "Here they are, boys! Three of them! Whoppers!"

We heard their mighty splashes as they came into view, taking herring on the surface like a trout takes a fly. We nearly wrecked the launches in our haste to get to them and tie up to our informant's boat. I will never forget the first sight I had of those tuna. They looked a thousand pounds, and even larger, when their blue bodies shot top speed through the water. They had not a jot of fear of us. Every time a herring was thrown over there was a mad scramble among them. They would dash toward us with terrific precipitation, then in a flash be gone, only to reappear a second later.

I shook in my boots as I watched them, and I know Z. G. was in a trance. Automatically he put a bait over and let it sink down about twenty feet. Captain Mitchell kept feeding the tuna, enticing them our way. There was a minute's lull, then a tremendous tuna came straight to the boatside after a herring. Z. G. yelled lustily. There was too much action elsewhere for him to keep his eyes on his own bait. I watched his line what times I could. Suddenly it straightened out, and Z. G. straightened with it. I thought he was going to catapult clear out of the cockpit. Quickly he braced himself and delivered a beautiful strike. We anticipated a terrific rush, but the tuna moved off leisurely, giving the boatmen ample time to set us free and start the engines.

Meanwhile the tuna fouled the line on a net buoy and things looked bad till Bob King cut the interfering rope. Then the fish woke up and went off like a shot. We increased our speed to meet his rate of travel. Z. G., in a transport of joy, held on heartily. Presently one of the small islands loomed like a live thing out of the fog, much too close for comfort. To all appearances the island was the tuna's objective. He swam fast some six hundred feet ahead of us, kept the line taut, and made the reel scream like an infuriated wind, and though we gained a bit on him we could not turn him from his straightaway course. Z. G. was saying nothing. He looked queer, smiled in a sickly way, and rested his rod on the ledge of the boat.

"Looks like it's all off," I shouted to the boys. "Can't you do something?"

The boat veered in a safer direction, but the fish would not give an inch. Before long he was sidling in the surf. My heart sank. There was no use trying to save him. He was a lost fish. Then, at the worst possible place, where I bade him good-by, he turned and headed out for deep water. What wonderful luck! I sat down, for my knees were too weak to hold me. After a while when the tuna took a breathing spell Z. G. bent his rod and back hauling in line. The sun, having partially dispelled the fog, gave us light and space to watch the tuna's antics. Sometimes he frisked on the surface, but more often he essayed long runs which gave Z. G. little chance to fight him.

However, by meeting his play with equal stubbornness, Z. G. in an hour's time had him within two hundred feet of the boat.

"He's tiring, sure as I'm born," I sang out. "You hand it to him now."

Z. G. laughed. "Yes? Wait till you feel the weight of one of these babies!"

Once I got a clear good sight of the tuna and I shouted my approval. I could not keep my eyes from him after that. He gave little line to Z. G. and took more than he gave. He led us a merry chase as far down the bay as he had worked up, and then aimed for the shore. To no avail did Z. G. try to coax him seaward again. He smelled land and the rocky buttresses and the backwash of the surf, and looked for protection there. I vow he knew what he was doing. Soon we were riding shorewise, darting around and between coastal boulders and rough rock. In his maneuvering the fish tangled the leader round his tail, but he suffered no dismay; rather, he grew more furious and determined. Doggedly he kept to the jagged boulders.

It was high time we thought of the boats and our personal safety. Even Captain Mitchell shouted a word of warning. There we were in water only fifteen feet deep, with the fish near but not within reach, slowed down in a confined area, but as full of life as he was when he first took the bait.

He worked farther inshore. Time and again the line slipped over rocks and threatened to catch. Repeatedly he turned and dove under the boat, forcing Z. G. to jump up and dip his rod in the water so his line could clear the propellers. Then he did it a last time—a fatal time. The line looped and fastened on the tip of the rod. When the weight of the swift tuna bore on it—snap! Another fishing adventure was done.

We were a pretty downcast crowd that evening. Z. G. seemed less disturbed than any of us. "Simply outfigured us, R. C.," he said.

At dawn the next morning we were on their trail again. Rain had fallen during the night and passed into a dense fog that made the early hour very uncomfortable. Feeling our way down the bay was eery sort of work, but we dodged the buoys and their *groaners* and located the herring fishermen without any trouble. Tuna were rolling near a number of the nets and it was only a matter of getting a bait in the water to have a tuna strike. At times the fishermen, to stave the tuna from the nets, themselves threw herring to them, and the tuna seemed to anticipate it and surfaced often. It was remarkable to see those monstrous fish rise for a feeding with all the ease and fearlessness of goldfish in an aquarium.

We tied up to a buoy. Z. G. put a bait in the water, and the next moment he had a terrific strike. We saw the tuna take the bait with a hungry grab, then make a dash for freedom. Line whizzed from the reel. The boys started the engines and we were after the fish without a minute's delay. Z. G. said later he had never experienced a more abrupt, amazing run. He was a new man today, enthusiastic, cheerful, full of energy, ready for any kind of work. The first run carried us three miles, and part of the time we were traveling full speed. This was merely introductory. On we went after the fish, off to sea in a fog, with bell buoys ringing and whistles blowing from every quarter.

The fight continued hour after hour; it was a contest of endurance, our speed boat giving us, I think, a little advantage. Z. G. never worked harder or better. He rose to the occasion splendidly, and though suffering from the strain of holding such an immense fish, enjoyed the prowess of his adversary.

After three hours we noticed some modification in the tuna's rushing tactics. He came to the surface far off. He took no rest, persevered at swimming, but seemed to have lost his assurance of victory. The fog had lifted and the sun was shining. We were miles off the mainland and going straight out to sea.

By the end of another hour Z. G. began to feel the wear and tear of the combat. The fish, now conserving strength such as he had put into his early violent runs, fought with a deliberate steadiness which permitted no minute of relaxation. He skirmished close. He would shoot over the surface, out of a great wake of waves and foam, describing a half circle as he came, then savagely shake his head and plunge back to his element, there to swim awhile before repeating his more active play. He did everything but jump. Such gameness we had seldom witnessed.

It was a fight to the finish. Z. G. at the close of the fifth hour feared it would be *his* finish. Anxiety wore so hard on the rest of us that we, too, felt fatigued. Fortunately the tuna was losing command and Z. G. stood some chance of winning. The plucky fish had taken us twelve miles to sea without once changing his course; but there was no safety for him in far horizons.

The sixth hour put Z. G. to a grueling test. When most tired, in order to avoid every possibility of disaster, he had to call upon his greatest skill and judgment. The end came suddenly. The tuna, after short jerky moves on the surface, surprised us by rolling over exhausted. Instantly we were on him. It was only a few minutes' work to gaff and tie him.

We came out of our bewilderment. Poor Z. G., who was limp as a rag, had to have his aching hand shook in congratulation by everyone within reach. Then we admired the tuna. Build and size alone declared him a real warrior of the deep. We could not tell his weight off-hand, but he was big enough to satisfy all of us.

Great was the commotion after we arrived at our mooring. It took five men to drag the tuna up on the beach. He seemed to increase in weight by the minute. Quickly we erected a tripod of three tall sturdy poles from which we extended block and tackle, and on this we hoisted the tuna. When his weight, 684 pounds, was announced, bedlam broke loose. Then, as excited and happy an outfit as ever drew breath, we photographed and rephotographed the victor and vanquished, so we might have for all time pictorial record of events of this glorious day.

Bad weather set in—rain, cold, and high seas. It was impossible for us to fish. For several endless days we went around chilled to the marrow, in oilskins and sou'-westers, and those nights slept in damp bunks and breathed thick fogs. Z. G. took it and smiled; he was in a mood to be gracious about anything. During our enforced rest, four tuna, of weights running around and above five hundred, were caught in the fish trap, while one big buster made a heroic getaway after smashing both net and weir.

As soon as the rain let up we took to our fishing again. Herring were thinning out and tuna were not so plentiful. We passed a couple of days without sight of a tuna. The market men said the storm had driven the herring out to deep water, but they would return, and with them the tuna, and both would remain till the spawning urge sent the herring traveling.

The third morning broke clear and bright. Fired with the promise it seemed to bring, we ran down the bay, only to find on arriving at the nets that the herring had not yet returned. Most of the fishermen had already gone for the day. We managed to pick up a few stray bait and forthwith started fishing. The water was dead. At nine o'clock we decided prospects were *nil*; however, we lingered for another half hour and were rewarded by a signal from a lone fisherman who had espied a tuna dodging round his net and very kindly kept him coming by tossing him a herring or two. We saw swirls on the water, but when we arrived old tuna was nowhere in sight. We waited for his return. Five minutes passed. We tossed over some of our precious herring. One after another they sank from view.

Then came a yell from Z. G. and a display of acrobatics which meant but one thing—a strike. He was hanging on to everything for dear life. The end of the rod disappeared underwater, the reel sang noisily, the boat moved away and we were off to battle.

This tuna took his time. He wove back and forth through the path of nets, missing all the threatening fouls, then wearying of that, gave us a chase up the bay.

Z. G. kept up a fire of enthusiastic shouts. We were all keyed to the same delight. Everything Captain Mitchell had said about these big tuna was true. If we had any fears that he exaggerated when he said he had hooked and lost as many as nine fish in one morning, they were dispelled now.

The tuna wove up and down the bay, and circled in and out, but never made an effort to go to sea. Excitement ran high. The tuna soon settled down to fight for honors, and so did Z. G., who was resolved to expend less energy this time than he did in the previous struggle. This fish acted much as the other had, only he put into steady pulls what the first fish had given to spectacular lunges. He gave us heart failure on his landward ambles, for fear he might get to the surf and rocks, but each time he turned and took a new course.

After an hour Z. G. observed that the fish was slowing down. "He doesn't seem to have the power of the other one," he declared.

No sooner had he spoken than the tuna, as if to discredit what Z. G. said, suddenly became enlivened and made some rushes across the bay that would have done credit to a submarine. Yet we gave him no chance to get very far from us.

"You've got it down to a system," said Captain Mitchell.

So Z. G. had, and the boatmen handled the launches more skillfully.

Z. G. worked like a Trojan. By the close of another hour the tuna was rapidly tiring. He was a good ten feet down when we ran up on him. He defied Z. G. to raise him, keeping at that depth while laboring slowly back and forth. He looked tremendous to me—much larger than the other one. I called the others' attention to this. Captain Mitchell agreed, but Z. G. was doubtful. Not long after that we gaffed the tuna.

We tied him up and then it commenced to dawn on the crowd that we had an exceptional catch. Z. G. took one long look and excitedly said: "Bigger than the other one! Longer, bigger around! What do you know about that?"

Our greatest surprise came when we tried to get him ashore and found it would take six men with block and tackle to pull him up on the wharf. There we got our first good look. We were staggered. Without hesitation Z. G. declared his tuna heavier than any fish ever taken on rod and line. Measurements were taken, scales adjusted, and finally the fish was weighed. A record he was! No one was happier about it than Captain Mitchell, who thereupon had to surrender laurels to Z. G. The exact weight of the fish was 758 pounds.

News of the catch spread rapidly. Spectators poured in from Liverpool, Shelburne, and towns round about, and newspaper men from as far north as Halifax came down to interview us. It was an immensely popular victory, and Z. G. received enough good wishes to last a lifetime.

Another spell of rain postponed further fishing. This we resented, for the tuna and herring season was almost at an end.

Finally the weather cleared. We were on the sea again, and it was my turn on the rod. The herring were running thick and the tuna were still with them. I was not kept waiting long. After I put a first bait over, Z. G. called my attention to a tuna he saw weaving our way, and while I was concentrating on his fish another snatched my herring so hard I was yanked to my feet. I had been told to strike the moment I felt a tuna take hold, but in this instance I did not have time. He was through with me before I was on the job. I rebaited and immediately made another clean miss. This was bad luck or very bad fishing, and I became overpowered with stage fright. Instructions from Z. G. and Captain Mitchell only fussed me more.

A third bait brought me another terrible strike. Forgetting my resolution to wait a little, regardless of instructions, I instantly pulled back on the fish with all my might. The hook held an instant, just long enough for me to feel a tremendous weight, and then pulled out. Then I *was* in disgrace! I had to take no end of reprimands without making defense.

The fish had scattered and gone to other nets. We had to scout around to locate them, which gave me time for reflection. I put my fourth bait over, firm in the intention to give my next fish a chance to swallow it. Along came a big fellow on track of some herring tossed over by a market man. He ignored the herring on my hook, but took everything else we threw him, so we tried tossing a loose bait and my hooked one together. He took the free one every time. I was on the verge of nervous collapse. Thoroughly exasperated, I let my bait sink down out of sight and waited. Suddenly he took it, but the shock was too much for me and so addled my brains that again I struck at once. The line quivered and the rod bent double, and on my second strike the fish started off like lightning. We took after him at once, and we were rejoicing because he was settling down for his first long run, when out came the hook.

I cannot describe the oppressive silence that followed this catastrophe. Nobody had a word to say. My teeth were locked hard. Darned if I wouldn't get the best of one of these beggars! I was too excited, over-anxious. I tried to simulate calm.

We returned to our first post and waited, but the tuna were not there. It was getting late, most of the market fishermen had gone away with their catches, and to all appearances fishing was over for the day. However, as had happened on former occasions, through the good graces of a kindly market man who still stuck to his nets, we had another try. It was a lone tuna, a straggler. We threw out a few herring which he followed down out of sight. I dropped a bait to a depth of ten feet. I could see it plainly. Below it came the tuna. At first he looked small, then gradually he looked larger. Up he rode, a glistening beauty, made a half turn on his side, and took my bait. I let my reel run free. He circled, then headed off. I saw the bait disappear in his mouth and a moment later I struck.

Instantly he set out on a terrific run. But no move was made to start the boat. There was a shouting of orders from everybody, followed by a wild scramble, and I thought I was outwitted again. I learned afterward that the propellers had caught in the eel grass. Though the delay was only a moment, I lost fifteen hundred feet of line before we were freed. We chased the tuna like mad for two miles without lessening the distance between us an inch, but after that I steadily gained on him. What a run! What an unerring flight! How he managed to clear all the herring nets is something beyond my understanding.

I worked fast and determinedly and pulled until I thought my arms would break. When I set the drag on my reel the tuna actually towed us. We wove in and out the bay, crossed and recrossed our tracks, and all the time I had to endure a terrible strain. I dared not ease up till I brought the tuna close. I planned to atone for the bungles of the morning, forgotten though they were now that a fish stayed with me. I gave him the best I had. Every time I weakened I drove myself with visions of him suspended from our tripod on the wharf. I fought relentlessly.

"Rome's not going to let this fellow catch his breath even for a minute," said Z. G.

My grim play might have accounted for the swift tiring of the fish. Forty-five minutes from the time I hooked him I had him alongside, and, instead of the usual resuscitation and fast fighting run which I anticipated, he rolled over like a log, belly side up. I pulled with all my strength. The boat slid over. Z. G. reached for the leader and with a wild yell gaffed the tuna through the mouth.

This sudden termination of the fight was the greatest surprise we ever had throughout our years of fishing. It seemed more incomprehensible later when the tuna was hauled ashore and found to tip the scales at 638 pounds. The baby of the three—yes! But he was my leviathan and for that reason seemed more beautiful than the others.

## CHAPTER IV

## MARLIN LAURELS

REMARKABLE luck and some very hard work fell to my lot the day I caught seven Marlin swordfish. It was in our early Avalon years when Captain Danielson stood by us at the wheel of the *Leta D.* through many a long hard fight. It was our custom then to make each season an ever happily anticipated trip to Clemente, an island some forty miles south of Catalina and more remote from the mainland. Clemente is a lonely, isolated retreat, volcanic in origin, a medley of mountains and crags, of cool green canyons rich with holly, wild lilac, wild cherry, and arbor vitæ and of golden oat slopes that are crisscrossed with thousands of sheep trails many a decade old. The sea and the rains and the wind have beaten great caverns in the rock walls of the ragged shore line. At the most habitable spot on the leeward side, a grassy bench at the end of a long white curving beach, a man named Pete Snyder kept a camp. There we lived and from there we fished and each evening watched schools of small bait skirt the shore to escape from feeding swordfish. Thus were we engaged the night before my memorable day of Marlin fishing.

We had had no good breaks to date, and Captain Dan and Z. G. were in most patronizing fashion putting it up to me to free us from the jinx. I figured a good run of flying-fish had intoxicated them with the idea of the morrow's possibilities.

I remember the next morning so well—cool, pleasant, with a blazing red sunrise and smooth sea. We were off early.

"Now it's up to you," said Dan. "A fellow with red hair oughter get these Marlin quick."

Danielson was a great soul. He loved to outfish other boatmen, and nothing pleased him so much as to put a large swordfish on the dock at Avalon. He was always the best boatman for swordfishing, keen for records and ready to stand by any angler with undying optimism. Z. G. was never shy himself at accumulating records and often urged me to try to wrest a few from him. I commenced to sense this fishing trip was planned for me and I was being jollied and encouraged with the idea that if my usual good luck prevailed I might achieve fame for all of us. I loved the fishing for fishing's sake, but I was always willing to do my best, and, being susceptible to suggestion and eager to please Z. G., I soon felt the desire growing on me to do something out of the ordinary. I had already taken Marlin swordfish heavier than 300 pounds, and it was a large order to ask me to do better than that.

We were looking for Marlin that last night had sent the flying-fish scattering like bursts of spray, not one Marlin but a school of them, for the flying-fish, obviously, had been attacked from all sides. With three teasers out and two baited lines we should have been able to fool at least a couple of fish. I made Z. G. agree to handle every other skirmish if we had a number.

Teasers of those days were flying-fish tied to short lines extending about twenty-five feet back of the boat, where they skipped over the surface of the water. We attempted to create the impression of a school of flying-fish swimming on the surface, and thus deceive the swordfish. We always ran our baits out beyond the teasers in the hope they would be sighted first. Often a swordfish attacked the teasers first, and then came a scramble to get a real bait to him.

[ 51 ]

On down the island we went. Dreamily I watched goats work their way over some far ridges, and followed the flight of an eagle. You cannot ride the waters of Clemente and think only of fish.

I was summoned back to business by a lusty yell from Z. G. Something had taken my bait. I let the line run free for a hundred feet, then struck hard several times. I rarely miss hooking a Marlin and I think it is because I strike repeatedly. It requires force to set a hook in a hard mouth, and far rather would I have a fish hooked in the mouth than have him swallow a bait, because that gives him a sporting chance to free himself early in a fight.

At the first leap of the fish I saw he was a small one, and did not anticipate much. I counted six jumps while Z. G. was trying to set his camera. You can always count on Z. G. for enthusiasm; no man on earth gets more thrills out of a jumping fish than he. The Marlin headed seaward, but I closed down on him and soon had him coming to the boat.

"He's not so much," Z. G. observed. "About one hundred and thirty. Hooked in the corner of the mouth. Not hurt a bit, Captain. Let's let him go. What do you say, R. C.?"

"It's all right with me," I replied, but I could see Dan was reluctant.

"Nobody will believe we caught the fish if we don't show him," he said.

"We'll take oath on it, Dan, if we must," returned Z. G.

Captain Dan cut the leader at the hook. The fish moved slowly out of sight, tired but not permanently injured.

Z. G. took to his rod again and Captain prepared me a bait which I carefully laid along the side of the boat.

"Hey! what's the idea?" my brother inquired. "You tired?"

"No, but I'm going to let you do the work now," I answered.

"Nothing doing!" roared Danielson. "This is a fishing-boat. Get busy and catch some fish while they're here. This starts like one of your days, R. C. Don't go turn it down."

I could not resist Dan's plea, so over my bait went. While I paid out the line a big Marlin appeared behind Z. G.'s bait. Z. G. yelled his delight, as he always does when a big fish comes round, and I felt my blood tingle.

We watched those darting fins intently. They made a quick flirting motion as the Marlin quit Z. G.'s bait and made a bee line for mine. I tried to reel in, but the Marlin was too quick. He grabbed my bait and started off with it. I hooked him in a jiffy. He threshed on the surface, then sounded, and left us to wonder where he had gone till in quite the opposite direction from where we expected him he commenced to jump. He wore himself weary. In fifteen minutes I was bringing him in with ease.

Dan reached for the leader and pulled him up. "What'll I do with this one?" he asked, belligerently.

"Cut him loose," said Z. G.

And that was that.

By the way he spoke, Dan must have expected this two-Marlin-per-hour consumption to keep up throughout the day, and all on one rod besides. I protested, and was sat upon, so out went another bait. The fights had carried us offshore some distance, but the Marlin were still with us.

Suddenly Captain yelled, "Look out!"

I looked up to see a big blaze of purple behind my bait. This fish was shy and careful. Circling round a few feet

[ 53 ]

ADVENTURES OF A DEEP-SEA ANGLER

from us, he looked the teasers over, but refused them, nor was he the least bit impressed when Z. G. jerked them into some semblance of life. I tried dropping the bait back of him. That availed nothing. After a few more merely inquisitive sallies he left us.

When Z. G. wound in his line a few minutes later I thought he wanted a new bait, but it dawned on me presently that he was laying his tackle away.

"Say, you can't do that!" I protested.

"Sure I can," he returned. "It's your day, R. C. I won't help you any if I stick a bait out there."

"It's not my day if I don't want it," I declared, stubbornly.

Z. G. grinned. "I've been hearing a lot about going day after day without getting bites. Now take your medicine and be happy."

He winked at Dan. It was a frame-up.

If I had debated with them longer I might have missed sight of a big tail that cut through the water behind us, and, strangely perverse as human nature is, the minute I saw it I wanted the fish to take hold. He was a whale of a Marlin, big, black, and hungry. He actually sprang at the bait. When he whisked round the water boiled. I hooked him immediately as hard as I could, and off he went like a streak. Captain took after him, whereupon he began to jump. What wild grace! What sure instinctive flight! I gave what strain I dared and so kept him within plain view.

Dan and I shouted in admiration. I could hear Z. G. snap pictures and toll off the jumps—twenty-three, twenty-four, twenty-five—up to thirty and over. I was kept busy handling the rod and reel and trying to save my line, but I saw part of the exhibition. Thrilling and beautiful it was. In all he jumped forty-two times. I brought him to gaff in twenty minutes after tremendous

THE FIRST SHOW

Marlin Diving

expenditure of strength. I was sweating profusely and realized I was tired out.

"This fish would go two hundred and fifty," said Dan. "Maybe we won't get a bigger one today. Better keep him."

"Let him go," was Z. G.'s response.

The Marlin was quick to realize he was free. He switched the water with his tail, swam off through the spreading ripples, and slowly sounded. Luckily, he was not crippled.

"This is fishing," said Z. G. "Three fish by ten o'clock. Let's see. That makes six before one o'clock, nine by four o'clock, and you might as well stick it out till seven and make it an even dozen."

"You've got the right idea," said Dan.

"A grand idea!" I averred, scathingly.

Then I groaned. So close to us that we could not possibly miss it, and ripping the water fast, was another fin. My body rebelled but my fingers itched. I had to shout the news to the others.

As soon as we circled him he rushed the teasers, and Z. G. and Captain Dan had a high old time trying to snatch them away from him. I reeled in my bait to a better position. He saw it immediately, and cut holes in the water trying to get to it. I hooked him hard and fast. This was to be a fight without quarter. Since my fellow musketeers wanted action, why not show them some?

At the finish of fourteen jumps, which he made in a circling run, I hauled the Marlin up to Captain Dan. I had pulled him in before he had a chance to retaliate, and he was not even tired. When Dan cut him away he darted down like a streak, too quickly for me to get a good look at him, but Dan said he was long and heavy.

Dan was jubilant. With speed that threatened apoplexy he rebaited my hook and tossed it over.

[55]

Z. G., meaning to congratulate me, thumped my tired back, and I gave vent to a few terse words.

The next fish came so fast I doubted my senses. There was no denying him once he had taken the bait. He looked like a barrel and was provocatively slow in his movements. After three or four half-hearted splashes he turned around, then, either frightened or hurt, he raced off toward the island. Dan, having no time to turn the boat, backed us into fair position.

Such a run! I felt my reel go hot. Instantly I tried to release the drag. It was stuck. Z. G. shouted to me, but I could not understand a word he said. At four hundred yards the line broke.

"Golly! what a fish!" I ejaculated. "Did you see him? Just feel this reel!"

That fish stimulated me. I forgot I was tired. I was keyed up for action. In ten minutes up came another Marlin and made for the teasers. We all pulled, but he grabbed them off—one, two, three.

"I never saw the like of it before," declared Z. G.

With a splash the fish took my bait. As he surfaced I saw the shiny flying-fish gripped tight in his mouth. At fifty yards he broke water, then, working the line over his shoulder, he started away in long bounding leaps and continued with a demonstration of lofty tumbling that left us gasping. Fast though he went, we kept pace with him.

There is a limit to human endurance. My second wind began to fail me. I ached all over; my back was strained, my hands were sore. What had been pleasure became an ordeal. It was impossible to appreciate the valor of the Marlin when I was wearing out.

I had no idea how long I was on the fish. I was victor in the end, but too tired to enjoy the victory. Maybe Dan was right when he said the fish would go a hundred and fifty. My aching muscles acclaimed him at least three hundred.

What next? I implored Z. G. to take the rod, but he was adamant.

"Something's going to happen yet," he avowed, bumptiously.

"Yet?" I echoed. "What more do you want? I'm nearly dead now and all you fellows are doing is having a good time."

Nothing I had to say counted. They baited for me, then went on watch.

It was hard to believe I had already taken five Marlin. One catch is usually called a good day, and if you are fortunate enough to manage two, a strut in your step is pardonable.

This day the Marlin were hungry and fearless. I do not believe it would have been possible to run one down and keep him down. When another came along I danced my bait through all kinds of antics to see if I could scare him. Nothing doing! He was determined to take it. I hooked him, and on his first clear-away leap I saw he was the smallest one of the day. This was encouraging—but only for a minute. What he lacked in size he made up in speed and endurance. He made twenty-two clear jumps, enough to tire a normal fish, and had enough fire left to chase far out to sea.

Wearily I hung on, wearily I worked. What a fighter for a little fish! I thought I would never land him. When I did, I, not he, was exhausted.

"Six," said Z. G. as Captain Dan took hold of the leader.

"Mmmm!" I assented.

"It's a record, R. C., and all let go alive."

So they were satisfied! I rose to stretch. Then I saw

[ 57 ]

Captain Dan go for my hook with a fresh bait in his hand. I glared at him.

"Aw, come on, R. C.," he coaxed. "You're not tired. Grab the rod and we'll cinch the record for once and all."

What was there for me to do but take up the rod?

Off the east coast of Clemente, my favorite place for Marlin swordfish, I revived a little and took some interest in my surroundings and dared to think we might have run away from trouble. At any rate, I had respite enough to review the day's events undisturbed and work up some pride in the laurels that had been forced on me. In time voices disturbed my meditations; first Z. G., "That's a swordfish!" then Dan: "No. Must be kelp waving. Too big for swordfish."

But Z. G. ordered the boat to slow up.

Enter R. C.!

An enormous body appeared like a shadow behind the boat, came to the surface, hit my bait, took it and faded away. The line slipped out easily for a distance and then stopped.

"He's let go," I said, feeling relieved.

"There's another," cried Dan.

The newcomer was a burly brute. He smashed the water mightily, on track of the teasers.

"Wind in your bait!" yelled Z. G.

I wound in slowly. My line bagged; something had my bait.

From behind me came Dan's stentorian shout: "He's got your hook. Had it all the time."

The Marlin surfaced suprisingly close. He *was* huge. He was champing on the leader. Having swallowed my bait, he was returning for the teasers. This fact was amazing to me. Without thinking of what I was doing, I wound up the slack line until it was tight and then struck with all my might. I realized instantly what a dan-

[ 58 ]

gerous thing I had done; I had struck a powerful fish while he was directly under the boat. Dan swore. Z. G., standing by with his camera, was going to make the most of a bad situation.

The water at our stern opened with a roar, and out of it flashed a magnificent infuriated Marlin, grandly savage and vengeful, who would have destroyed us if he could with the wash of waves he threw over us. So near he was I actually smelled him. The next two jumps we could not see for water. I heard Z. G. and Captain Dan shout instructions, but I was too dazed to heed them. On the next intimate leap the Marlin shook his head like a demon. He went down, disappeared, and after a brief spell charged us again.

Dan shouted to me to take care, and at the same time pushed the boat full speed ahead. The swordfish smashed into the water, then rose up under fresh propulsion till he stood before me on his tail, his great body wagging and blood streaming from his mouth. Dan gave another warning cry. I was too excited to care, too paralyzed to move. When collapsing from the caper the Marlin pitched himself across our stern, striking the hull of the boat just low enough to prevent him from tumbling aboard. We were drenched through and through and the cockpit was full of water. In his next two jumps he missed us by a yard. As we turned off, he circling one way, we another, he bumped us amidships, and that sent him moving. He passed somewhere under us, grating my line on the bottom of the boat so hard that I thought for a moment the end of the fight had come. His furious rushes had been a matter of a minute, yet in that time he could have wrecked the boat.

At safe distance from us the Marlin swam heavily. His worst surface work was over.

"I knew how easily something like that could happen," ejaculated Dan.

Z. G. looked a bit shaken. He said he would take happily to the sea any time a Marlin heaved himself aboard. I had not thought of any of these things, but had sat mute and paralyzed, with a slack line on my rod.

It took me two hours of the hardest, most relentless kind of labor to subdue this fish. He was too heavy to lift aboard, so we towed him back to camp and later took him to Avalon, where he tipped the scales at 328 pounds.

Once the ordeal was over, though I was tired beyond words, muscle-bound, and aching in every joint, I was heartily pleased that Z. G. had bullied me into the very exceptional achievement of catching seven Marlin swordfish in one day.

CHAPTER V

## MORE SWORDFISHING DAYS AT SAN CLEMENTE

BACK to the island of green-gold slopes and hidden glens where flowers grow unseen!

That was the burden of my song on August 19, 1920, when Zane and I, astir in the gray light of dawn, were hastening with the final packing for our annual San Clemente trip from Avalon. By making an early start we could avoid the late morning westerly wind that daily churns the channel between Catalina and Clemente, and arrive in good time.

At six-thirty we set off from the Tuna Club dock in the *Blue Finn*, Captain Sid Boestler's thirty-eight-foot V-bottom boat, which, equipped with an engine that made fourteen miles an hour, cut down distances for us. Sid, in his pleasure and enthusiasm at the prospect of fishing with us at Clemente, could scarcely wait to cast off.

The morning was clear and cool, the ocean calm and smooth as far as the eye could see. Passing Pebbly Beach, we almost ran over a large Marlin swordfish. He was looking for something to eat, but we could not take advantage of that, as we had no tackle ready, a lucky circumstance, no doubt, for the joy of a Marlin fight would have outweighed the fear of a rough channel. We watched his angry splashes and the scattering flying-fish that marked his course, until he was lost to view.

At Seal Rocks we counted thirty seals, among which were several large ones. Some were barking from the rocks, others riding the swells or lying on the beach. The Austrians had been caught taking seals in their nets and we feared this might mean extermination for the friendly mammals that for so long have been a source of interest and pleasure for Catalina tourists. Their ranks had thinned.

A couple of miles off Seal Rocks we ran into a heavy swell and the *Blue Finn* rode up and down like a cork. Z. G. and I were out on top, watching the waves and the long, continuous heave. Many a happy hour we have spent this way, many a wordless hour when silence was the keynote of sympathetic companionship. The ocean with its changing moods, its pervading mystery, its eternal tragedy, and its opportunity for conquest, has had a tremendous effect on my brother's development. Often in these silent hours he is going through the pangs of creation or is suffering the struggles of some phantom creature who lives in his imagination.

We kept an eye out for swordfish, and when we sighted a fin or saw a fish leap in the distance, we argued on the possibility of its being a broadbill or a Marlin. Often in our days on the sea we have pursued a Marlin which we first saw leaping far off, and when we reached the spot found the last dissolving spots of foam where he had disappeared and perchance got a strike. But Marlin and broadbill were safe in our company this day. We resisted the temptation to bait our tackle.

While we were engrossed in scanning the sea, a large school of porpoises headed for us, making the water boil and the spray fly with their long bounding leaps. We jumped for a camera. They came on, saw the boat, and veered past, a few staying on the surface as they went by. It is remarkable how fast they travel and it would be interesting to know how far they can go in a day.

We could not locate any schools of tuna, but we saw large flocks of gulls and ducks. If you go out for tuna, such a sight is cause for rejoicing, for usually where gulls and ducks are bunched tuna have been feeding. These

R. C. with 328-pound Marlin

The "Gladiator" at Clemente

birds get most of their food by following the schools of feeding fish, and we can thank them for many a tip.

Wherever we sighted floating kelp we were sacrificing a strike. Under it sometimes you find a Marlin, often yellowtail, and always small fish.

As we neared the middle of the channel we spotted two whales blowing ahead of us and we followed in their wake for a long distance. One finally sounded, the fluke down broadside, and we cheered him for the fine display he gave us.

After passing the middle of the channel the sea grew calmer, and two hours later, in the lee of Clemente Island it was smooth as a floor. I fell into thoughtful anticipation of the many delights Clemente offers: swimming in the clear cold water that laps her shore, exploring her caves, climbing her oat-covered hills where flocks of sheep scatter before you, beholding the splendor of the Pacific, its fogs and dawns and sunsets, from stands where eagles circle in lofty flight and solemn ravens croak their "nevermore."

My brother pulled me out of my reverie with the words, "Hey, Red, there's Pete, waving his arms like a lunatic."

Pete was at the edge of the beach, zigzagging like a sailor in distress. His life was little less lonely than that of a man marooned. It was only during two months of the year that sportsmen visited the camp at Clemente. An occasional fishing-boat came to anchor there during the other months, but such visits were few and far between. Pete met us in his rowboat, put us ashore, and helped transfer our luggage. We were glad to see camp, glad to be comfortably installed in our tents.

Before supper we had an invigorating swim, then we sat down to a generous repast which we tackled with a will. Not long after, snug in our blanketed beds, we were lulled to sleep by the song of the surf whispering its secrets to the shore.

The following day was one of adjustment and preparation. Show me the man who could resist the charm of Clemente—she is an Undine to a fisherman. You revel in her charm and forget the purpose of your journeying.

We spent the morning exploring the ever-new island. I was sorry to find some of the sheep dying. A very light rainfall the winter before had made the water-supply scant, and the tanks in the canyons that held the yearly yield for the sheep had gone dry. Only those sheep that had returned to the ranch, Clemente's one other inhabited spot, were saved from suffering or death. Clemente has her tragedies. Not so many years ago, Dominquez, the old Mexican sheep-herder, as rugged and stern in his age as the island coast, had been found dead on one of the trails, a victim of a bullet accidentally discharged from his own gun which had dropped from its holster.

In the afternoon we took a swim and tested the condition of our fishing tackle. Everything had to be in A No. 1 form, for our hopes for great fishing were high.

That evening we set a net for flying-fish, something a local Marlin fisherman had to do every night if he would keep himself supplied with fresh bait. The procedure is interesting enough to bear explanation. Just before dark you set the net, a regular gill net, about two hundred feet long and four feet high, placing it a short distance from shore. Lead sinkers at the bottom anchored it securely, and large corks at the top acted as buoys, keeping the net taut and preventing it from sinking under the surface. As darkness gathered, flying-fish tore their way toward shore to escape larger fish that came up to feed, and they ran head first into the net. The mesh of the net was just large enough to permit the head to go through. The fish could struggle no further, because

[ 64 ]

of the increasing bulk of their bodies, nor could they pull back, owing to the spreading of their gills. Some nights they came in thousands; in a few minutes you had a couple of hundred fast in the net. Other times they came in lesser numbers, and now and again there were none at all. When the fish were scarce it was wise to stay with the net, going over it every few minutes. Occasionally a neglected net was destroyed by seals that became entangled in it while trying to steal our captured bait. It was weird work to ride near your net on a dark night when the sea was rough. Often the flying-fish leaped over the boat and sometimes they struck you as they passed.

The day had been of that delightful order typical of Clemente in August—early morning foggy and cool till the sun's reaching rays, pushing the mists apart, spread their glorious light and warmth; early afternoon enlivened by a mild westerly breeze that came down the island to play on the water a few hours, quieting as the red and gold of sunset touched the sky and dying with the light to perfect calm; then evening with the fog returning.

Z. G. was up at the break of the new day, and when I rolled out he was off down the beach, searching for shells and singing lustily. I intended to take a swim before breakfast, but the temperature of the water at six A.M., when the air was cool and a fog cloaked the rising sun, was a little too low for me. I changed my mind and was satisfied with a brisk rubdown. We had a good breakfast of grapefruit, cereal, bacon, eggs, cakes, and coffee. Pete always was a generous provider, believing a man who fights big fish needs nourishing food.

We left camp at seven with a goodly supply of the flying-fish we had caught the night before. It was foggy and cool, with the water very calm in the lee of the island. Off the west end it appeared rough, which gave partial promise of a stiff wind before the day was over. We put out three teasers and two baits and trolled down the island, where we tried several of our favorite fishing-places. The Haunted Rock and the Glory Hole, both famous spots, were quiet. Since you were always informed of the presence of a swordfish by frantic efforts of flying-fish to leave the immediate vicinity, we knew better than to waste more time there.

Next we ran off the east end of Clemente and made several large circles. It was here I caught the largest Marlin of the year 1916, weight 304 pounds, and again the record fish of 1918, 328 pounds. A long run up the west side of the island to Smuggler's Cove and China Point, without a sign of life, made the outlook discouraging. It was now past noon, warm and clear, with a faint breeze coming up. Z. G. and Sid had gone on top to talk and to look for fish. They usually did shake me when the fishing was slow. They planned new baits and new ways to attract fish, and left me with two rods and three teasers to watch. This may not seem like much of a job, but I have seen some funny and several heart-breaking things happen under such circumstances. A charge of a couple of swordfish or big yellow-fin tuna would usually clean out all the baits before anything could be done.

I was dozing in the warm sunshine when suddenly I was wakened by a resounding splash. It seemed as though some one had fallen overboard. I looked in time to see a teaser disappear and a huge swordfish diving at another one. I yelled lustily for help, at the same time winding in my bait and trying to keep the teaser from being snatched. Z. G. and Sid came tumbling off the top, inspired by my yell, and attempted to help. The advice offered to me was great, but I could not follow any of it.

BIG MARLIN WITH DORSAL ERECT

Z. G. AND FINE CLEMENTE MARLIN

Sid threw flying-fish overboard, hoping to keep the Marlin on our track.

Z. G. yelled: "Wind in! . . . Let out! . . . Can't you see you're doing it wrong? . . . Get it in front of him!"

I was trying all this. But it was the swordfish's game, not ours. Anyhow, he had no intention of leaving us. After leisurely eating several flying-fish that the captain had thrown over, he finally found my bait and slowly sank with it. I hooked him, and when I felt his tremendous weight I realized that I had a large fish and that a difficult task was cut out for me.

He started away, leaving a broad wake in the water as he turned. He was slow and heavy at first and cleared the water only enough to let us see that he truly was good size. He worked offshore, going slowly to sea, and grew faster and stronger as he went. We followed him for a long distance. Then he sounded. I pulled with all my strength for an hour, trying to bring him to the boat. We saw him several times. He would come within fifty feet of us and then stop. He kept this distance, and I could not gain a foot. It might have been that he wanted to look us over, as they often do. By this time we were three miles off the island, with the wind coming up and the sea getting rough. The fish changed from heavy plugging to fast surface work, going into the sun and wind. This made it difficult for me. The bright glare of the sun was so blinding that it was hard to discern the line. Either I was weakening or the rough water and wind were aiding the fish's escape, for he kept moving faster and kept widening the distance between us. We ran after him, trying to get the sun at our backs, but he outwitted us.

Two hours passed. I felt disaster coming. I hated the sun, the wind, and the waves. I was suffering all over. My arms and back were giving out. All this time Z. G.

[67]

had stood near me, offering what help he could through suggestions, and Sid did his best with the boat.

This fish was not for me. I felt it. In making a long fast circle he got a bag in the line, gaining too much slack, and at that came straightway for us. It was impossible for me to take in the extra line rapidly. On he rode. Like a shot he disappeared under the boat, then cut the water on the other side. I jammed the rod over and down as far as I could reach, the one and only thing I could do to save the line from the propeller. No such luck this time! The line caught, snapped—and my agony was over. I was tired out. I sat down with a sigh, wondering how it had all happened. I knew I had made my mistake in working too hard the first hour. No doubt about his being such a large Marlin, and hooked in such a way— probably in the corner of his mouth—that he escaped without injury. His real size or the particular fashion in which he was hooked are things we will never know, but to me he seemed larger, stronger, and faster than any Marlin I had ever fought.

We cut the water toward camp, Z. G. repeatedly stating, by way of encouragement, that I had done well with odds against me.

August 22nd dawned. Z. G. called me early and I woke with stiff muscles, sore back, and stinging, paining hands. I was tired out and wanted to rest. The idea of a quiet day under our sun-shelter with a good book had a strong appeal. But when I was told I was getting tender and could not expect to handle large fish much longer, I decided to limber up a little and go along. I took a painful but invigorating swim, bathed my hands well in the salt water, tried a few setting-up exercises, and felt better as the result. I showed up at breakfast full of enthusiasm.

Old Sol appeared early and called forth a happy mood with his cheerful glow.

My secret prayer and desire as we put forth in the *Blue Finn* was that Z. G. would have all the luck and do all the fishing.

A short distance from camp we sighted a Marlin and speeded up the boat to overtake him. On the way another Marlin came up behind us and took a teaser before we could pull it from him. We let the first fish go and turned our attention to the second. He dropped back a little and took Z. G.'s bait. Z. G. made a clean miss of him, and while he was winding in to prepare another bait, the Marlin took mine. I also missed him and was much surprised to see him return for more fish. He appeared a bit wary, trailing us at a distance. In the meantime I baited again, and when I cast off I laughingly remarked, "Watch him take this one!"

Sure enough he did! He deliberately crossed from behind Z. G.'s bait to take my flying-fish. This time he sped away in a business-like manner. I set the hook hard and he commenced jumping at once, and he did some marvelous leaping and tumbling, clearing the water thirty-six times before he settled down to fight it out. Z. G. had several good chances for photographs while this jumping was going on.

Well, the joke was on me! I would rather have been the witness of the battle than the participant. It was not long before I was hot and tired.

Every new fish has a method of fighting all his own. This one tried weaving back and forth a short distance behind the boat for over an hour. It was a wearing-out process, but I began to gain a little. The advantage was mine from then on. By degrees I drew him close till I had him where Z. G. could reach him with the gaff. In short order we had a rope around his tail. We weighed the Marlin when we reached camp. He balanced the scales at 165 pounds.

Our third day's fishing was attended by good luck from its very beginning. The minute we started away from our mooring Z. G. sighted a Marlin, and soon after we saw two others tearing through the water for something to eat. Before we could head them, one came up directly under the boat and took a teaser. Then he grabbed Z. G.'s bait and started away with it. Z. G. hooked him without any effort. I was ready with a camera, looking for a picture on the first jump.

Z. G. handled the fish with great ease and in fifteen minutes had him near the boat. The fish had jumped about eighteen times on his first run. We tried to get him to perform near the boat, but he had jumped his last. Evidently he was tired out. We got him aboard, a fine 135-pound specimen.

"How about hooking a whale today, Rome?" suggested Z. G. "You look as if you could tackle anything."

"Sure I can," I replied, glibly. "You pick him out and I'll do the rest."

We went around the east end of Clemente, seeing several Marlin on the way. They followed us, but ignored our baits. The wind was blowing there and beating the water. We welcomed this condition. One of the chief delights of a Marlin seems to be to ride the waves.

Far ahead I saw two fins coming nearer and nearer with steady swift movement. The fish made for my bait without any dallying, and crushed it off without giving me the slightest chance to hook him. Soon after another made a play for the teasers, but Z. G., by quick maneuvering, tempted him to his bait. He hooked the fish and it cut madly through the water. After four leaps the hook pulled out.

Presently a big fish charged Z. G.'s bait, cleaned the

hook, and made for my bait. A minute later he was hooked solidly and making fast for the open sea and rough waters. His jumps were magnificent—nineteen frantic infuriated attempts to throw the hook. Then he took a series of long plunges, gaining line all the time, until he was almost a thousand feet away. We ran after him and he sounded as we came. For two hours and five minutes I fought him with all my strength. Three times he had been near the boat, each time darting away with renewed vigor. I conquered him in the end. He was a fast, strong, 284-pound fish, and in the splendid fight he had showed, he had taken us almost five miles offshore.

On the 24th I landed a 150-pound Marlin after a forty-five minute fight. He cleared the water thirty-one times in his effort to get away. It was late in the afternoon when I hooked him. It had been a clear, warm, delightful day, with the ocean smooth and swordfish scarce —one of the days when you spend most of your time atop looking for fins that fail to appear.

Our gala day came on the 25th. The day began with a mood that pleases the Marlin—a steady wind and rough water—so up they came early to ride the waves and snatch a breakfast. Shortly after we put out I counted five of them frisking on the surface.

"Take your pick, Rome," yelled Z. G. from the top, where he stood bracing himself against the stiff wind and reveling in the stirring scene.

"You can have what I leave," I conceded, graciously.

Then with some remark about coming to take advantage of my offer, Z. G. swung down beside me. Later, when I had hooked one of the fish to have him shake me after a dozen splendid jumps, Z. G. said to Captain Sid, "He's a boastful customer, but he can't make good."

In a very little while Z. G. suffered the same experience, and Sid exclaimed with unconcealed disgust: "Looks like you're two of the same kind. Better do more fishin' and less talkin'."

I cannot say whether or not it was the result of this advice that before long I was listening to the hum of my reel and watching my taut line widen the distance between me and a leaping fish, but it had happened and we were all on the *qui vive*. He cleared the water nineteen times and made a nineteen-minute fight. At the end of that time Z. G. had a gaff in him.

"Twin brother of yesterday's fish," said Z. G., falling just five pounds short in his estimate.

Before noon was on us Z. G. had a fifteen-minute fight with a frisky little devil who made thirty-six jumps. He was a 75-pounder. Z. G. looked at him somewhat disgustedly and said, "Of course he's a fish, but I'd give a lot for a whack at a man's-size one."

Since we had been heading out all morning, I suggested we try the east end of the island for a change. The wind had grown stronger and the sea was running rougher. Occasional fins reminded us that the swordfish were delighting in this day. They were sportive, appearing one minute, disappearing the next.

We were trolling off the east end when a yell from Z. G., coupled with a sudden threshing of the water, brought me to eager attention. Just beyond Z. G.'s bait, leisurely riding the waves, was a husky Marlin. He passed back and forth a few times near the bait, with the reserve of a cat with a mouse he knows is his for the taking; then he pounced on it. When he lit out he convinced us that the rougher the day the more active the fish. He seemed to glory in the fight, seemed to know that with the sea so riled the odds were in his favor. He postponed his jumping until he had given us a lively chase. Twenty-six admirable leaps he took, and meanwhile the boat

[72]

pitched unceasingly. I sat down hard once when I had neither the desire nor the intention.

"Hey, Rome! stop rocking the boat!" yelled Z. G., gleefully. "Can't you see I'm having a hard enough time with this load of dynamite?"

After forty-five minutes' work Z. G. brought the Marlin to gaff. I never have been fond of gaffing fish when the launch is teetering like a seesaw. However, the job seemed to be mine. I chasséd around the cockpit in great style. When I did get the gaff in the fish he gave one wag of his tail that yanked me so hard that only special favor with the gods saved me from the indignity of being hoisted aboard with a grappling hook. There were some tense minutes before we had the fish secure, because he backed his resistance with 290 pounds of brawn.

The fish had headed us seaward again and we kept the course, moving slowly. Z. G. had only a short respite from toil. Another Marlin came his way and took his bait without coaxing. He was brought in after thirty minutes, during which time he made twenty-four attempts to toss the hook. He weighed 175 pounds.

On the way in, I hooked a Marlin that was averse to accepting my company. He leaped a half dozen times, so I could see he was fairly good size, then left me. This had been a great day. We had taken four fish, hooked three others, and had some wonderful opportunities for pictures.

The sea was so boisterous the next morning that we voted to stay in camp and enjoy the luxury of a lazy, restful vacation.

Another day brought a heavy fog and perfectly smooth sea. We rigged tackle and teasers with fresh flying-fish and ran down past the Glory Hole and on out to sea beyond the east end of the island. The fog had lifted at ten o'clock and the weather turned warm and radiant. We made several turns around the east end, but with nary a sight of a Marlin or a thrill of a strike. About a mile out we encountered a stiff breeze blowing down the island. We trolled for three hours and not a fin cut the surface anywhere in that time. Off Smuggler's Cove a number of flying-fish were jumping in fevered haste, but since there were no signs of swordfish we concluded yellowtail were chasing them.

On our return to the east end, about one o'clock, I saw a large fin, which on first sight I mistook for a broadbill's, and found afterward belonged to a Marlin. From a distance I could not determine whether he was feeding or playing. I tried every conceivable way to get a bait near him. No success! Several times we got dangerously near him. He had no fear of the boat. Time and again he went down, only to return alongside us. For thirty minutes we played around, trying to tempt him to strike. At last, by making a short turn, we cut off his advance at a distance, and I placed my bait about fifty feet in front of him. He was traveling fast. He saw the bait, went under, and a moment later struck it with his bill. There was a tense second. I scarcely breathed. Then a welcome jerk on the rod and the zumming sound of the reel! He went slowly, taking a long line. I struck hard. Immediately the line slacked and I thought he was gone. But when I wound in I made a sudden and joyful discovery—he was hooked, hooked and coming toward us. The boat moved slowly. The fish slipped up alongside and looked us over. He lingered a minute, then turned and started to sea. He surely could speed, and he employed tremendous power with graceful ease. We ran after him. He jumped several times and fooled us with some incomplete leaps. After a while he turned out from

[ 74 ]

the rough waters of the east end and headed toward the lee water. This was fortunate for me.

Several long runs, eight threshing leaps, and one hour of pulling and pumping brought the Marlin in full view near the boat. It was only for a minute. I could not hold him. At the end of the second hour I had him up to the gaff, badly spent. We tied his tail and towed him five miles back to camp. There we looked him over. I figured his weight at 350 and fell short very little. On the scales at Avalon, after loss of blood and considerable shrinkage, he tolled off 354 pounds.

It was a great disappointment to me that, by a careless oversight on Sid's part, my big Marlin was cut up early the next morning before any photographs could be taken.

August 28th ended our 1920 season at Clemente. It was a great day, with the ocean alive with swordfish. Z. G. took two fish, one 175 pounds, the other 165 pounds. The first fish made fourteen leaps, the second thirty-six.

The only chance I had at a Marlin I missed. It was in the early afternoon. I saw one coming toward us, pushing something ahead of him and creating a violent disturbance in the water. I wondered at his antics. Then, as he came near, I saw he had a large bonito in his mouth which was struggling to get away. We ran up close on them. The Marlin let the bonito go and sank under the boat. I watched the bonito. He started away lamely, scarcely able to swim. Showing deep in the water under us was the purple of the Marlin, gradually growing more distinct as he neared the surface. He did not seem to mind the boat. He came up beside it and then swam leisurely after the bonito, as if he knew it could not get away and he therefore was not called upon to hurry. I saw him take the bonito and with it slowly sound. I was

[75]

so intent on his performance that it never occurred to me to pass him a bait.

The following day we returned to Avalon to lay away our fishing-tackle. Always when I go to Clemente I strain my eyes for the first sight of her lonely shore; always when I leave her green-gold slopes my glance is backward till distance veils her from view. Those who have been there cannot fail to understand.

CHAPTER VI

THE TREAT OF A SEASON

AFTER the severe strain of three months' broadbill
fishing—June, July and August, 1923, at Catalina—it was not to be wondered at that Captain Sid and
I rather loafed on the job, so far as actual yearning for
big fish was concerned. But Z. G. was relentless and indefatigable; he did not intend to call the season closed
without some smashing climax. During the last eight
days of August, which saw the end of our broadbill
swordfishing, he made us drag the teasers and keep a
bait out all the time, on a chance of getting a strike from
a Marlin.

Throughout the entire month we had seen only three
Marlin, small ones at that. As August is the usual time
for their appearance, we were of the opinion they would
not come this year, or else would come very late. As a
matter of fact they did come late, in October and November, a run of small fish.

Dragging flying-fish teasers twenty to thirty feet behind the boat is no trouble or work, and to have a rod
tied in the chair, with a bait out and a thin thread barely
holding the line is not difficult. But here comes the
rub. Somebody has to keep a hawk-eye on the bait
and also the teasers, because a Marlin can slip up and
steal any one of the three very easily, which means
opportunity lost.

Since Z. G. and Captain Thad spent most of their time
atop the deck of the *Gladiator* or in the crow's-nest on the
lookout for broadbill, it fell to Sid and me to keep an
eye peeled behind for Marlin. As for Sid, he had gotten

to the place where he might have seen a flock of whales, if they had jumped on the bow of the boat, but he certainly could not have seen a Marlin. Sid's eyes and nerves were worn to a frazzle after three months' Z. G.-ing over the ocean. As for me, I had my sight left, but the rest of my strength was shattered. I wanted ease, a chance to hide away from the glare of the sun, an opportunity to seek some retreat, luxurious and shaded.

Every morning, when Sid procrastinated over the teasers, he would swear and say: "Aw, there ain't any Marlin comin' this year."

I was of the same opinion, and stronger in the belief that if they did come we would not see any. I had made up my mind to pack away my tackle the evening of August 31st.

Well, the day arrived, and Z. G. celebrated it by catching his third broadbill of the season—360 pounds. We were jubilant. The long drill was over.

"Tomorrow is September first," remarked my brother, complacently. "One more day, just for luck, we'll go for Marlin. *Quien sabe?*"

So that was how we happened on the next day to be on the distant, windward side of the island, off Catalina Harbor. It was afternoon, hazy, warm, with the mountains lost in fog. The first breath of a westerly wind rippled the dark blue water. Sid was asleep at the wheel, Thad was in the chair on deck, facing the bow, and Z. G. was in the crow's-nest. I sat below in the cockpit, half asleep, with one partly shut eye on the blue water astern. I was drowsy; I had to rouse myself every little while. There were moments when teasers and bait and the ocean itself were a blank to me. After one such spell I imagined I saw a shadow moving back of the flying-fish bait, but I often had such hallucinations and thought this was only

[ 78 ]

another. However, I was not too sure. Presently I sat up to grumble, "Darned if that doesn't look queer!"

The shadow was green and silver. It loomed up behind the bait, and it weaved to and fro. Then it showed the widespread purple-colored pectoral fin of a Marlin. Once seen, those fins could never be mistaken. It was a monster Marlin. Like a shot I jumped up and yelled at the top of my lungs:

"*Swordfish!*"

The great body rolled up to the bait the very second I broke the thread and let out the line. When I straddled the rod and grasped it the Marlin had taken the bait and was sheering away, flashing like a broad shield.

I heard a yell from Z. G., then a thump on the deck. He had jumped or fallen out of the crow's-nest. Sid and Thad came running, but did not beat him to my side. It certainly was a thrilling moment. The line ran steadily off the reel. I looked up at Z. G. and gasped, "Did you see him?"

"I sure did," he flashed back, his eyes bright and smiling, as he watched the line slide out. "Whale of a Marlin! Grand strike! Let him have it a little longer."

But I shut down on the drag and jerked with all my might, wound fast and jerked again till the line came tight and the rod bent and bowed.

"Soak him a couple," Z. G. called out. . . . "There— that bird is hooked. Of all the luck! . . . Say, who was it made you drag teasers and a bait? Huh!"

We all became intent on the line. The fish did not run or come to the surface, as is usual with Marlin. He moved away slowly and heavily, taking perhaps fifty yards more off the reel. He was describing a semicircle.

Sid indulged in a play of enthusiasm and boasting most remarkable, considering how he had kicked on fixing the teasers and had sworn the Marlin species was extinct.

[ 79 ]

Thad was interested; he had heard enticing stories about Marlin, but he had never seen one.

I began to feel an excitement incident to a hunch that a heavy Marlin is about to leap. But when the fish came to the surface, about two hundred feet from us, all he did was stick his bill out. He moved very sluggishly and hardly made a ripple.

"He's tangled his tail in your leader!" exclaimed my brother. "The son-of-a-gun can't swim!"

So indeed it appeared. Several broadbills had been caught foul-hooked this way by other anglers, and we saw at once what a deadly business it must be for the fish. Sid and Thad made most interesting comments.

Suddenly the Marlin made a motion like a diving seal and sent waves broadening in every direction.

"He's freed his tail!" yelled Z. G. "Look out now! Where's my camera?"

Pyrotechnics began. I felt them telegraphed up the line to my hands. The Marlin rose to the surface, shot ahead in white foam, went down with a rip, then once again split the water with a loud crack, and leaped magnificently, a huge, broad, glittering silvery-white purple-striped fish, sight of which was enough to make anyone yell. We all yelled!

He made eleven such leaps, indescribable acrobatics that must be seen to be appreciated; then, turning, he came back broadside to us, thundering and crashing the water. There was a big bag in my line and I pumped hard to lessen it. But his speed kept the line tight.

"He's getting close!" shouted Z. G. "Oh!—I've shot my last film!"

Such was the luck of it. The Marlin turned straight toward us, and as if to give us the thrill of our lives leaped prodigiously. This time it was Thad who shouted loudest.

"Throw in your clutch, Thad," ordered Z. G., sharply. "Quick! Full speed ahead!"

The propeller roared, the *Gladiator* glided forward. The fish showed his broad white belly, in his up and onward surge. It seemed sure that he would hit us. Like a shell from one of the great man-of-war guns, he ricocheted on the surface and made the water fly. He passed us ten feet astern, churning the sea into a huge patch of white foam, and then plunged down.

Z. G. was breathing hard. "Wow! Are you all here?" he managed to articulate. "Get back in your chair R. C., and down to business."

Apparently there had been no slack line, but I declare it was not due to any skill on my part. I pulled and wound. After a time the Marlin came up, perhaps fifty feet from us, and stuck his head out of water. His jaws were gaping.

"Look at the hook—look at it!" groaned Z. G. "It'll drop out!"

The bright shiny hook protruded from the upper jaw, so shallowly imbedded it must soon be pulled free. It was a disheartening sight. Sid swore and Thad snorted. No longer had I hope of landing the fish.

"Keep your line tight, but not too tight," admonished Z. G. "Handle him very carefully."

It was easier to be the man standing by than to be the man in the chair, yet I know Z. G. suffered from apprehensions no less keen than mine.

The Marlin was out of sight again. He sounded a short distance; I gave into him a little and checked him a little. I put great stock in my magnificent tackle, a good old Murphy hickory, special twenty-four-thread line, and a 9-0 Coxe reel. I invoked its loyal support. It seemed to respond.

[ 81 ]

The fish did not show on the surface again, nor did he do any fast work. He swam off to sea and we followed.

In something over two fearful hours I had him coming and saw the end was close, the point where either he would shake the hook or be captured. I had expected the first alternative every moment since we saw where the hook was hanging.

Sid, who was cold with skepticism, said, "Wouldn't it have been great to take that fish back to Avalon?"

"He gave the grandest exhibition I ever saw," returned Thad. "I was sure glad to get a look at one of them, anyway."

Throughout the ordeal Z. G. stood beside me, camera in hand, silent and doubtful, yet holding to our one chance. At last the wonderful silvery white and purple colors began to flash through the green water. I had the Marlin coming.

"He's licked, R. C. Now if the hook only holds!" said my brother.

I eased the Marlin in under the slightest possible strain, and presently he weaved and rolled on the surface near the boat. What a fish! What a game adversary!

Z. G. snapped out orders to Sid, who had grasped the leader. "Let it slip through your hands! . . . *Hold* now! . . . Watch out! He's rolling this way! . . . *Pull!* . . . Grab your gaff! . . . Make sure! . . . Careful!"

It took all of us to pull my prize on board, and I had to confess he was larger than I had guessed. But even after seeing him I fell far short in my estimate. Z. G. came closest with 310 pounds. This Marlin, a particularly graceful and shapely fish, weighed 324 pounds! No sooner did we load him on the boat than the hook, without being touched, fell out of his mouth.

Perhaps it would be well to note here that at this time I am the only angler with more than one 300-pound Cali-

A Marlin Swordfish on the Rampage

R. C. with 324-pound Marlin

fornia Marlin to my credit. I have brought in five. If you took issues on it with Z. G., he would say: "Sure, the lucky devil! A Marlin can't resist him." Nevertheless, they were captured at the price of stiff relentless fights which won from me the highest respect for the *Spearfish* family.

We brought this splendid specimen in to the dock on a holiday. Avalon was crowded with Labor Day excursionists, and between four o'clock in the afternoon and nine that night upward of ten thousand people took the trouble to go out on the dock to see him. Many were tourists from remote corners of the country, and their expressions of wonder and delight were indeed something to remember.

CHAPTER VII

## THE CONQUEST OF THE BROADBILL

IN THE summer of 1916 I made my first visit to the Pacific coast. I located at Avalon, Catalina Island, where one lives close to both mountains and sea, and was immediately charmed by the beautiful resort. It has the most delightful climate the year round of any place I know, little rain and prodigious sunshine tempered by cool early-morning fogs. The air is fragrant with the scent of sage and eucalyptus, and gold of wild oats glisten above the brilliant blues of the bay. Peace, beauty, and the vast Pacific! The ocean with its long rolling swells affected me profoundly.

My dream of a decade had come true. Gone were the years of fishing on the Atlantic, where I was tanned and light-seared and blistered, and my patience and appetite continually threatened by rough waters. Although I confess my discomfort, I do not mean to belittle the good I gained by persevering. I was rewarded with many a thrilling adventure and a splendid broadening of knowledge of life in the sea. As I look back upon daring encounters with big sharks, tuna, sailfish, and many small varieties of fish no less interesting than their larger kin, the hardships I bore became insignificant. And, after all, it was the complete revolution of conditions that made my Avalon experience surpassingly pleasant.

In August that year, while fishing as usual with my brother, I saw for the first time a broadbill swordfish. Z. G. paid great tribute to this royal monster of the deep and he assured me I was in for a surprise. Daily he scanned the ocean, trying to find one. This fish, like the

Marlin, when swimming on the surface shows the dorsal fin and the upper part of the tail a foot above water. In angler's parlance searching for these fins is called picking them up. No one could beat Z. G. at that trick of the sport. On this day of great occasion he showed me specks in the distance, calling them fins of a broadbill, and it seemed incredible that he could identify them correctly so far away. But such they were, and as we ran up toward them their motion indicated a weaving, milling creature idly sunning himself. I was amazed at his size. He was fully twelve feet long, with a body as round as a barrel, a large round eye which seemed to follow your every motion, and a long, broad bill, sword-shaped and most murderous-looking. After one glimpse of him I laughed at my brother's suggestion that *I* play a broadbill. It would be enough to catch a Marlin, I figured, and tuna fishing took my time as well.

Four years passed during which I captured a fair number of tuna and Marlin. There was no longer any excuse for me to evade the broadbill game. After observing my brother's battles, I was really eager to try a hand. Wherefore, one day, accompanied by Z. G. and Captain Dan, I put out with purpose to pick up a broadbill if one had the good grace to make his presence known.

I was left in the cockpit to do the fishing while the others scattered to scan the sea. We ran east around the island toward Catalina Harbor. This had always been a favorite course for tuna and Marlin, and sometimes a broadbill showed.

The early morning was cool, with fog, but as the day advanced the sun shone bright and the sky and water became a beautiful blue, and a mild westerly wind raised little white caps. Hours passed uneventfully. Along toward noon we all grew indifferent. Z. G. dozed in a chair

[ 85 ]

on the cabin-top and Captain Dan assuaged his impatience by smoking one cigar after another.

My memory does not need the jogging of a diary to recall that at eleven-twenty, after a bored consultation of my watch, I looked up to see far off the black gleaming fins of a broadbill. The realization of that moment will stay with me forever. Captain Dan was startled by the shout I gave, and Z. G. sprang from atop to the cockpit. Immediately business picked up; Z. G. prepared rod and bait, Dan ran the boat toward the fish.

When Z. G. handed me the rod I noticed my hands trembled. Fine state of affairs, I thought, for a man who always approached his fights with tuna and Marlin with keen delight! My nerve was good and my physical condition splendid, but the sight of that dorsal fin and the powerful easy motion of the tail awed me. I think I had a premonition of what was about to happen.

Z. G. climbed back on top the boat to direct the placing of the bait before the fish. All this time I watched the broadbill swimming slowly on the surface. The closer he approached the larger he grew. He was long, of good bulk, with broad shoulders. His eye seemed at moments to defy me; again he drifted lazily, careless of our approach. I was not feeling very gay, to tell the truth. My adversary was much too sure of himself.

As my bait, a large flying-fish, passed about fifty feet in front of him, the broadbill flirted his tail with a nervous motion, speeded up, and heading straight for the bait sank from sight. I sat silent. A strange anxiety possessed me. Would he strike or not?

Minutes passed. I began to feel relieved—freed from the agony of anticipated conflict. Then suddenly the line whipped from the water. I felt a hard blow at my bait. Having been informed that the broadbill usually strikes the bait from three to four times before taking it, my

BROADBILL FINNING

This Hooked Broadbill Whacking at the Leader

senses were acute to receive new shocks. They did not come, but my line quivered.

"He's got it and leaving!" I yelled.

Z. G. stood beside me, and Captain Dan behind. The line slipped away, gradually speeding up. I was enthralled. I was powerless. A broadbill, my first one, and with a bait in his mouth! I watched the line pay out in wonder.

Through my strange stupefaction came a chorus of yells from Z. G. and Dan, "Hook him! Hook him!"

I came out of my trance with a shock. I set the drag. The line straightened instantly with a tremendous check. I struck with all my strength. The line twanged tunefully. Watching in fear, I struck again and again. Everything held.

Little more than one hundred feet away the water opened. I saw the flash of a tremendous body. Momentarily the broadbill stood up, massive and terrible, threshed back and forth, and then sank slowly from sight.

A sensation of weakness came over me. I felt insignificant, impotent.

Z. G. was very sympathetic. "Take your time, old boy," he advised. "It may last quite a while. Seems as if you're tied to a big one, so don't use up your strength early."

Perhaps in my eagerness I disregarded what he said. I gave away not an inch of line, except at what seemed the breaking-point. I pulled with all my might. The fish fought slowly and heavily, now and again raising his body half out of the water, which he threshed to foam. His broad bill wagged back and forth. Z. G. and Captain Dan said things incomprehensible to me in my fierce concentration; I gave no heed to them nor the passing time.

I had a triumphant sense of strength and kept a powerful strain on the rod. At the end of an hour I had the fish coming—slowly but surely I was bringing him to the boat. At forty feet I saw him distinctly. Long, with great purple-hued body, he looked his rôle of gladiator of the sea. I pulled, using every ounce of force I had. The double line came over the reel and the twelve-foot leader showed in the water. The distance between me and the fish did not exceed twenty-five feet. I could scarcely believe my eyes. The fish watched me, but did not seem frightened.

Here was my chance! I yelled for Z. G. and Dan. "Grab the leader! Gaff him!" I called in desperation.

They shouted back: "Ease up! Ease up or you'll break the rod!"

Such instruction seemed unreasonable, but I could not help giving in gladly to anything that meant relief. My thumbs were paralyzed from shutting down on the reel. I saw the double line fade away. The fish moved off and out of sight. It was heart-breaking. I sat in a daze. I felt at once that my only chance of getting the fish was gone.

The broadbill's reaction to the change of circumstances was displayed in new tactics. He tried heavy runs, traveling like lightning in strange bursts of speed. We raced over the water, back and forth, chasing after him, but we did not gain anything; as much line went out as I took in, and neither of us had the advantage for long.

At three-thirty, after hours of fighting, I was in a deplorable state and commencing to break under the strain. I was close to exhaustion and it was very difficult to accept the truth, because I had been so confident of my endurance. I asked Z. G. to take the rod. He refused. "Something might happen," he said. "Stay with him."

I laughed at the courage my brother entertained for me. I knew there was not a chance in the world. Only the man at the rod can judge the weight of his fish and be first informed of his weakening. This fish was fresh, getting stronger and braver, and taking pains to show me that my four hours of pulling had been ineffectual. Small wonder this was so! He was twice as large as any fish I had ever landed.

Goaded by a forlorn hope, I fought on madly. I wanted to do well, to be game, as they say, but I was working against terrible odds. I weakened as time passed, and after five hours and forty minutes I had just enough strength left to pass the rod to my brother and stagger to the cabin, where I sank down on a bunk, miserably sea-sick, utterly exhausted, completely whipped.

But my interest in the fight was still keen. Miserable as I felt, I leaned out of the bunk to keep an eye on Z. G. He was having his good time feeling the fish out. He cast a backward glance at me that was more expressive than words. I gathered that he, too, considered this fish un-beatable. I *knew* it was beyond human strength.

It took an hour of clever work to bring the line's hun-dred-foot mark in sight, yet the admirable effort counted so little against the grim determination of the fish. He dragged the mark back into the sea. Two hours of re-sistance availed nothing for my brother; gradually the broadbill gained on him, taking line which, as the fight progressed, was getting harder to recover.

The sun set, twilight came, darkness settled upon us, but the fight went on. Indistinctly I could see the move-ments of the men outside. At seven-thirty I saw Z. G. pass the rod to Captain Dan. In my weakened and help-less condition such a move was a joy to me. Only an angler who has had difficulties with large fish and had to stand the scorn of his boatman—for all boatmen think it ought to be easy for an angler to bring these fish in—can appreciate the situation.

The captain worked, swore, and puffed from exertion,

but he did not make the slightest impression on the broadbill. After two hours he conceded that he had never felt anything more whale-like, and yielded over-quickly to Z. G.'s suggestion that he take a hand on the rod with him. They pulled and worked together.

Finally the reel wore out. The drag gave way. Relieved of the strain, the swordfish woke up and ran wild —short runs, long runs, surface fighting with much splashing of water. The sound of battle was weird in the dark of night. Then came delicate spattering from everywhere and I saw against the sky, in the gleam of the deck light, a silver flash. Flying-fish!

I heard a streak of profanity from Dan, followed by a hearty chuckle from Z. G. My nerves were raw.

"He's chasing flying-fish," I yelled. "Better give it up for the night, boys."

Sure enough! That was actually happening. Hooked as he was, and after three of us fighting him for over eleven hours, the foxy unbeatable old broadbill was feeding on flying-fish and having a grand time. It was too much for Dan. I learned afterward that at once he pointed the rod straight out, held to the line and purposely let it break.

That for me marked the beginning of many broadbill swordfish fights. Thereafter no fish interested me as much as these did. I fished patiently day after day through good and foul weather. If an angler has to make a catch every day to keep up his enthusiasm, he had better not go after broadbill. Ordinarily they are hard to find and that summer they were not numerous. I fished into September without hooking another one.

A year passed, and June of 1920 found me back on the job. I had trained all winter to get into condition for what I knew would be a hard season.

On a warm and foggy morning in late June I picked out a broadbill for active combat, as active indeed it proved, but why I chose such a whopper I do not know. Fate has a way of leading me to the big fellows, never to a nice 250-pounder which in those early days was the peak of my ambition. Yet I was not turning away from any fish, no matter what his size, so I fed the newcomer a barracuda. He refused that, then I tempted him with a flying-fish. The way he rushed to take it without striking was a delight to behold. I hooked him and very soon discovered he was a surface fighter. He had plenty of speed and went everywhere. He seemed to know the ocean was a big place.

At the end of five hours I managed to get the broadbill close enough to the boat to see that the hook was at the outside of his mouth where it could not hurt him. This probably accounted for his wild antics on the surface and the fact that he never seemed to tire. After six hours and thirty minutes the hook tore out and he went his way. I had stood this long fight better than my memorable first. I was learning to conserve my strength.

During the later part of July my brother hooked and landed a very fine broadbill after one of the greatest fights I have ever witnessed. A beautiful fish it was, 418 pounds, and the largest of the season.

We seemed to play turn about in fighting fish. July 23rd was my day. I found a big broadbill, showed him my wares, and without hesitation he took what I had. He struck the bait a couple of resounding raps and promptly walked off with it. It was so simple to hook him that I feel sure he swallowed the bait, which confession betrays the tragic ending of the story. I felt his weight for a short time, then, without my bearing any unusual strain on the rod, the line broke. I saw a flash of purple, and peering over the side of the boat watched the broadbill cross our stern at top speed, my line trailing after him.

August came on with lovely warm days, but the month advanced unfruitfully, and I grew desperate for action. Was I to pass through another season without catching a broadbill? This miserable thought persisted. Days grew monotonous—stupid. The delightful weather changed. Heavy seas sent us homeward early many an afternoon. I was near to the quitting-point. Z. G. stuck it out with me day after day, and his cheery companionship and ever hopeful attitude were the only things that bolstered me and kept me from flunking. Whenever he found a fish he insisted that I take the rod, though I would protest there was a spell on me which kept fish from my bait.

When one day late in August I had the good fortune to hook another broadbill, I accepted my brother's, "There! I told you!" with great equanimity.

This boy came to the surface and stayed there most of the time. We chased him back and forth. He took line, but I recovered well. Since there was nothing startling about his size I seemed to stand a chance of landing him. I played him with great confidence. He seemed so surely mine when I brought him to the gaff early in the fight, but as the boatman struck, the fish gave a powerful lunge, filling the cockpit with water, then tore free. This was not as discouraging as it first appeared. The fish was badly injured, so he could not last long. After I worked on him another while he returned to the boat, and this time moved so slowly that we could see the leader was caught in his tail and the hook was outside his mouth. We could not avert the tragedy. The leader slipped off and the fish sank slowly out of sight. This crushing defeat ended my broadbill fishing for 1920.

## THE CONQUEST OF THE BROADBILL

The summers of 1921 and 1922 tested my patience and endurance to the limit. I had six broadbill fights, the shortest of thirty minutes' duration, the longest ten hours and ten minutes. Disaster seemed to follow me. Then, too, I made many mistakes and was unfortunate to hook up to the very largest fish. After hours of hard work something would break or the hook pull out. I went through my stern schooling day after day, week after week, season after season. What kept me going was the thought that luck would change, for the average was surely in my favor, and I must be patient for another while.

I had been fishing all of June, 1923, and part of the following month, spurred by good weather and a broadbill sea and fins of tantalizing fish that had no use for my baits, when one day, in the middle of the channel between Catalina and San Pedro, after working seven broadbills, I at last got a bite. Good old number eight! He hit my bait a terrific blow, grabbed it, and started away in earnest, slowly at first, but soon whipping up to lightning speed. I knew what that maneuver meant. He felt the hook and was going to jump, and a jump so early in the game through my experience had invariably been fatal. He would leap beautifully and throw the bait and hook!

I jammed on the drag and struck as hard as I could and at that was yanked forward in my chair. Looking up, I saw a most magnificent swordfish, fully fifteen feet above the water, curved like the letter S, shaking himself violently, and six feet to one side, high above him, I saw my barracuda waving. The broadbill crashed down and then came out in his second wonderful leap, this time making a complete somersault. I could do nothing

[ 93 ]

but look on. The reel burned my fingers, the line sagged.
I sat dumfounded. On his third jump, a still higher one,
I nearly collapsed. Z. G. had fallen off the top of the
boat, shouting wildly for a camera. Captain Sid was awe-
struck and neither moved nor spoke. I felt an unwelcome
relief from the terrific strain. The line went slack. I knew
at once he was gone.

Dejectedly Z. G. climbed back to the crow's-nest.
Maintaining an injured silence, I prepared another bait
and then held it idle. It was not long until Z. G. called
out: "Hey there, Rome! Another broadbill! Straight
ahead!"

I had no hope, no anticipation regarding this one. Me-
chanically I put the bait overboard, after the fashion of
one who does a thing expected of him. The boat circled
round this newcomer. On the very first turn he flipped his
tail and went for my bait. It was only a moment before
he struck. Z. G. tumbled down beside me. Again the
fish struck. There was intense excitement, excitement at
its breaking-point. We waited for the third strike. It
came, electrifying me from top to toe. The line paid out.
I let him take plenty, then struck hard several times. He
surfaced in a great splash of foam. We yelled. At last,
thank fortune, I was hooked on again, the second time in
one day!

I worked recklessly and I shouted defiance when he
plowed near us. Again and again he leaped, a jumping
broadbill and solidly hooked. I could not believe my eyes
or the play of my muscles. I lent all my strength to the
task. Time sped by. I felt singularly able, not tiring,
not aware of the strain. After long spectacular action
the fish slowed up a little.

Z. G. stood by. "Your turn's come, old boy," I heard
him say.

This Is the Eleven-and-one-half-hour *Xiphias Gladius* That Got Away

Z. G. Congratulating His Brother on His First Broadbill, 400 Pounds

With grim concentration I endeavored to justify that speech. The hours were annihilated one by one. Only vaguely was I aware of their passing. I remember fourteen jumps. I remember the broadbill stayed on the surface near the boat for a long while, so close I could see him and every movement he made, and I thought he was there an eternity.

When I espied the wire leader in my brother's hand I wanted to shout, but was voiceless. He lifted the fish a little, then not daring to lift any more, had to give way to the fish and let the leader go. It was terrible for me to watch that leader slip from sight. I imagined the things that could happen, considered the nearness and yet remoteness of victory at such a crucial time.

I pulled the fish up again. We suffered the same experience. Again and again it happened. Every time I saw the leader leave Z. G.'s hand I nearly died. At last he hung on. I watched him gradually raise the fish, and all the work and suffering and disappointment of other occasions defied me to expect the best. A terrible moment it was. Then Captain Sid reached carefully over the side and heaved toward the boat with a terrible pull. A mighty wave of water showered the air with spray. Was it true that the gaff was holding? Yells of joy from Z. G. answered that. While Sid cinched the gaff rope on the side of the boat and Z. G. bound a rope around the broadbill's tail I clung dizzily to the rod. I was afraid I might wake up and find it a dream.

When I accepted my good fortune as true, I cavorted about the launch surprisingly lively for a man who had just spent four hours and twenty minutes on the rod. If you want to turn back to the abandoned glee of youth, go catch your first broadbill.

The swordfish weighed an even 400. I can see him now,

[ 95 ]

hanging from the scales, outlined against the blue of sea and sky, and I live again the thrill of that conquest.

There were many conquests to follow, but the recounting of some of those, and among them my greatest, I must reserve for the climax of this book, for I consider them the greatest victories of my fishing career.

ꞁꞁꞁꞁꞁꞁꞁꞁꞁꞁꞁꞁꞁꞁꞁꞁꞁꞁꞁꞁꞁꞁꞁꞁꞁꞁꞁꞁꞁꞁꞁꞁꞁꞁꞁꞁꞁꞁꞁꞁꞁꞁꞁꞁꞁꞁꞁꞁꞁꞁꞁ

## CHAPTER VIII

### FOLLOWING THE PACIFIC

IN JANUARY, 1925, I embarked for Balboa with my brother, his son Romer, and some friends, there to meet the *Fisherman*, my brother's "ship o' dreams." What Zane had coveted as a boy was realized at last—he could roam the Seven Seas in a white-winged schooner that was his.

The promise of the prelude trip aboard the steamer whetted our zeal. Off San Bonito Island we saw a whale, blackfish, and a school of porpoises and small fish jumping, and birds flying back and forth over them. At Magdalena Bay, which is 750 miles from Los Angeles, we sighted broadbill swordfish bound for winter quarters; to what part south we could not tell, but have always been anxious to determine, for it is possible that Magdalena Bay, where broadbill are seen in great numbers at all seasons of the year, is a spawning-ground for these swordfish. We counted twenty-four broadbill in those waters and we must have missed as many more. Sharks, seals, and whales showed there, too.

As we continued our way south we met schools of small flying-fish, brown fellows and pygmies compared with our Avalon variety. Along the coast of Guerrero, old Mexico, 600 miles below the Gulf of California, Z. G. identified sailfish fins, some of which I at first mistook for Marlin fins. They were sailfish, but of such size and length as to deceive a man acquainted only with the Florida species and unaware, as indeed ichthyologists were, that the sailfish inhabits our Pacific waters. A Florida sailfish measuring seven feet in length is considered

[ 97 ]

a large one. These were unquestionably ten and eleven
feet long. One proved its sprightliness by jumping clear
of the water twenty-one times. We cheered him.

The steamer, running about ten miles offshore, kept
in sight of the mainland all day. The low country along
the shore was brown, parched, and barren, but the lofty-
peaked mountains that reached to the sky for rain were
covered with great forests.

Another day we passed some lonely islands which, in
the bright light of the afternoon sun, stood out pure white
against the dark background of the coast. Upon inquiry
the captain of the ship told us they were called the White
Friars and were the homes of millions of gulls and booby
birds, and little did we guess at the time that that name
would one day be for us the key word to extraordinary
fishing memories.

In these waters were many loggerhead turtles, on
whose broad backs black and white gulls rode, with no
fear of being molested by their carriers. There were small
snakes in great numbers, black with stripes of bright
yellow down their sides, and a good two feet in length.
It seemed to us unusual to find so many snakes so far offshore, though the sailors reported them common to that
locality.

We passed the volcanoes of San Salvador, some of
which lighted the night with flaming spouts of red, then
within two days we were crossing the Gulf of Tehuante-
pec. Here we ran into a southeast storm and got our first
touch of real rough water, the steamer diving into big
waves, pitching and tossing and throwing spray over the
bow and decks.

After nine days' sailing we reached the Canal Zone
and docked at Balboa. Far into the great bay of Panama,
on the south side of the water that forms the narrows to
the canal, stands the beautiful government-built town.

Approaching Cocos Island

FISHING AT COCOS ISLAND

Hummocky mountains, emerald green with vegetation, roll into gray distance on both sides of the silver belt of water which divides two continents. Such is the prospect from Balboa, a town of many levels and winding roads, with white buildings and red roofs and a luxuriant tropical background which was then in a riot of colorful bloom.

I was a proud American when I viewed the operations at the canal and realized what a gigantic engineering feat it had been.

We visited Old Panama. Among the ruins we felt the romance of its history. One could almost see Morgan, the pirate, chopping his way across Panama, building bridges as he went, pillaging and destroying the city, and taking with him all its rare treasures and jewels.

The *Fisherman* had made a record run from Lunenburg, Nova Scotia, its home harbor, and was ready to receive us and leave on a minute's notice. The ship was a fisherman's home—sturdy, neat, comfortable—not a luxurious pleasure yacht. It had been reconstructed to fit our purpose, had new engines and fine, full sailing equipment.

January the 30th we set sail from Balboa for the Cocos Islands. With wind behind our sails we rushed through big waves and white water, and we were being breathed into rocky motion by the time night came on. I had to cling to my bed now and then, but I got some sleep after midnight. Early in the morning I was awakened by resounding splashes along the side of the ship. Looking out my porthole, I saw blackfish jumping everywhere. They followed us for hours in most playful spirit.

We rode a calm sea that day, so we had no use for sails, but we made good time traveling on our power. Though the weather was hot, we kept comfortable under awnings spread fore and aft over the decks. There were a few signs of small fish surfacing. Trolling from the ship with a hand line we caught a dolphin of about thirty pounds.

At twelve o'clock on February 3rd, Z. G. from the crow's-nest high up in the rigging, sighted Cocos Islands and heralded the news with a shout. It took us all afternoon to run in. Small fish broke water as far as we could see. There were schools everywhere, and big splashes at intervals assured us of large fish. We ran back and forth over the schooner, as thrilled as a crowd of youngsters, claiming attention for each new captivating sight, exclaiming, yelling, and thumping one another heartily.

Hundreds of birds met us far off the islands and escorted us in, and when we dropped anchor they took immediate possession of the ship. They seemed pleased that we had come. Few were the times they had seen ships anchored there. The majestic mountain island, with its impassable jungle growth, its flowering brush and trees, and the long, white-gleaming crescent beaches belonged to them. They nested where once stealthy pirates trod searching for places to hide their loot. Yet for all the beauty surrounding them—fairy glens carpeted with ferns and deep soft moss, vistas of deep-blue water, crystal clear, caught through the graceful languid palms, and mountain-tops that challenged them to highest flight —the note of their little lives was tragedy. Where the booby and frigate bird live together there is no peace.

The frigate bird of the Cocos Islands lives by robbing the booby bird of its feed for its young. He is coal black, the male of the species marked with red, the female with white. He is swift and graceful and has a great spread of wings. As a flyer he is world-famed. The booby bird, dark brown in color, with feathers soft as velvet, is also a great flyer, but does not compare with the frigate bird in speed.

It is all in a day's work for a booby to travel two hundred miles to sea. I have seen hundreds of them returning late afternoons from their far-away pursuits. Always as they approached the islands a cloud of frigate birds, so dense that it darkened the sky, would move out to meet them. Then strenuous combat raged. The air would ring with screams and the fight grow fiercer and fiercer. The booby birds would dart to and fro, trying to outfly their enemies and reach their hungry fledglings. But what chance had one booby against the merciless onslaught of a dozen frigate birds that one after the other would pounce upon her from above? Exhausted by the struggle, she would at last disgorge the fish she had fetched for her young, and a frigate bird, swift on the wing, would catch the prize before it struck the water.

I watched these encounters in anger and disgust. I hated the frigate birds. Yet such was their struggle for existence. Only a few boobies got their precious cargoes to their little ones. I saw an especially wise booby bird outwit her pursuers by alighting on the water and ducking part way under, which so provoked the frigate birds that they quit her for a minute. When they renewed their attack the booby bluffed them again and she persisted at this game till they gave her a fair field for flight. Could she have known that once the frigate bird soaks his wings he is trapped and cannot rise?

On shore the booby retaliates by fighting and killing the young frigate birds, whose mothers, though they will strive to shelter their babies, will never attack an intruder. Thus does nature strike a balance in the struggle.

Our first night at the Cocos Islands revealed our anchorage to be far different from the peaceful place we had imagined. The *Fisherman* rocked continuously, sails flapped and anchor chains groaned. From the shore came the eery cry of an owl. Our isolation became oppressive.

At dawn the screams of countless birds brought me out on deck. The air was fragrant with the scent of wild flowers. A heavy dew, thick as rain, had washed a brilliant finish on the foliage of the island.

Over the side of the ship, where the deep-blue water was penetrable, I watched a pageant of sea life, vast numbers of fish—small brown turbot lined up with white, red, and yellow snappers—under them crevalle, mackerel and wahoo, and farther down yellow-fin and Allison tuna, and beneath the entire congregation indistinct brown shadows that were sharks.

The fish were not disturbed by the presence of the sharks. What I observed might well have been a happy family gathering. There are times of peace in the sea, yet I feel that its creatures are always alert for the inevitable hours of strife.

I thought of my boyhood days when, with a thread for line and a pin hook, my greatest ambition was to catch stray sunfish along a quiet stream. And here were legions of fish! I called Romer and his friend John Shields, who came rubbing sleep from their eyes.

"Talk of fish!" I ejaculated. "I guess we won't lack for something to do here."

Romer peered over, then he gasped, and forthwith the boys made staggering plans to annihilate all these species. Zane joined in the confabulation. "Well, son," he concluded, "guess I picked out a good place this time. You expert fishermen will look like amateurs before we're through here."

We set out that morning to explore the island beyond the stretch of beach. It was not long before we discovered that the Cocos Islands were populated with wild pigs.

Owing to the heavy underbrush and thick vegetation, it was almost impossible to see, but we could hear them scamper at our approach. Z. G. would not let us risk a shot. He reminded us of the time he had wounded a wild pig and was promptly surrounded by a furious family, against which his rifle was of so little avail that he had to take to a tree for safety.

Romer loved exploring, but, boylike, just at this time fishing was his dominant thought. His dad and I were keen to enjoy the shade of wide-spreading coconut palms and watch lazily the flight of the birds. However, we gave Romer's desires preference.

When we disembarked from the *Fisherman*, the one small launch we took was loaded with all of Romer's equipment—rods, reels, lines, gaffs, spoons, and a dazzling display of artificial baits, besides numerous devices unfamiliar to me. Z. G. and I each took one light tackle outfit in case between Romer's spurts we got a chance to fish.

Z. G. tinkered with his rod. I remained in the background to await developments. Romer, though only fifteen, was not a novice at fishing. He had several kinds of game fish to his credit and knew what it meant to fight a heavy one. He inclined toward tackle a little too light to please his dad and me, but we knew bitter experience would be profitable for him, so we offered no suggestions. I enjoy light tackle on light-tackle fish, but it is out of place in water where leviathans swim.

Romer put a spoon over and turned to us with a bright smile. "Some place, Dad! I'm sure glad you brought me!"

Our idea was to run up along the shore for a while. We did nothing of the sort. We stopped dead and stayed dead, for Romer had a smashing strike which we saw threaten him, a fifty-pound jackfish that came like a hungry wolf. Just the one lunge and it was all over! Romer's

[ 103 ]

spoon was gone and his line broken. Out went another bait. Smash! Bang! Again he reeled in a hookless line. Action continued fast and furious. Romer did not rest a minute. He lost bait after bait, broke rods and wire leaders, and caught fish to his heart's content, regardless of wreckage—yellow and black spotted jacks, many varieties of grouper, cero and Spanish mackerel, crevalle and snappers.

All these fish were abnormally large for their species as we knew them. Mackerel ran to fifteen pounds, the others to forty, fifty, and sixty. Hundreds of sand sharks, four to five feet in length, were themselves active in taking baits. Strangely enough, they did not molest our fighting fish.

Romer was in his glory. His clothes were wet and torn, and blood bespattered, too, and he reeked with the smell of fish, and he slid about the cockpit on scales and slime, but still he fought, still he had not had enough. No parlor fisherman this lad! Dirt, blood, sweat, work gave him savage joy.

I could not keep out of it. I dropped a cut bait overboard and let out a little line. Frigate birds tried for it, so did something from below. I saw a flash of yellow and after that my rod bobbed and my line paid out with a song. I was hooked to a speedy fish. Did I stop him? I should say not! The line ran from the reel until it smoked, and before we could turn the boat 450 yards of nine-thread line were gone, snapped from the reel at the fastening.

With a wink for Z. G. I said to Romer: "That didn't look much like a light-tackle fish. What do you suppose it was?"

Romer was much too busy to reply.

Z. G. got curious then. He took up his rod and grinned

THE FRIGATE BIRDS STEALING OUR BAITS

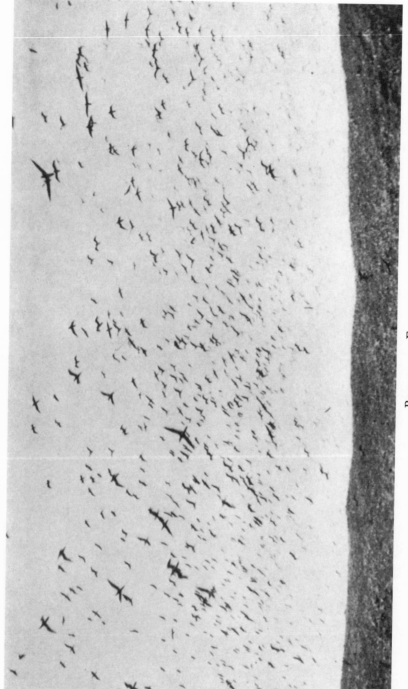

BOOBIES IN FLIGHT

at the six-ounce tip. "Guess I'm losing my mind, but here goes," he said.

He dropped a bait overboard. It did not last a minute. I tried to see what took it, but it was too quick for me. The fish broke the line.

We were now well offshore in deep water. One by one frigate and booby birds dropped from the sky and skimmed the sea for our baits. So many followed they became a nuisance. Some got entangled in our lines and others hooked themselves before we had time to pull our baits away. Fighting flying birds on light tackle was a new pastime, but we did not favor it.

They drove Z. G. to change his bait to a feather jig which did not interest them so much. Almost at once he was hooked to a fish. Wild as the rush was, somehow he managed to end it before all his line was gone. I vowed the fish was a tuna because he fought deep, as Catalina tuna do. Z. G. played him for a half an hour. He bent the rod almost double, tried to break it, I think, but did not make much of an impression on the fish. It was hot. Perspiration rolled from Z. G. in streams. He handed me the rod. "Take some real exercise, R. C.," he admonished. "You need it down here to stay well."

I was not anxious. I do not care enough for light tackle on heavy fish, but I was willing to have a try at it.

Romer prodded me a little. "Pull 'em up, Uncle Rome. Show Dad how to do it."

I pulled and pulled. Nothing doing! There was no use trying to raise that fish. He weighed a ton. I worked to break the line, but everything held. Then my rod wagged violently. The weight trippled. There was a rush. A larger fish had come along and given the *coup de grâce* for me. I wound in what was left of the line.

We turned toward the *Fisherman*. Romer continued to fish, but Z. G. and I were satisfied for the day. The lad was quickly busy again. He hung on with all his might, thumbed the reel and checked up the fish only within a few feet of the end of his line. This was a real fight. Patiently and carefully Romer handled the light tackle, rescuing it from the breaking-point many times. At last he brought the able fighter to the boat.

"Kingfish!" we yelled.

But no! We were wrong. It was a wahoo of forty pounds, big and beautiful. We had caught wahoo in the Gulf Stream off the coast of Florida, but nothing so large as this, and we were surprised to find them so far from the habitat with which we were familiar.

Romer's glee was great. "Why, I could fish here forever, Dad," he declared.

Early the following morning I trolled down the island, keeping well offshore to avoid the smaller fish. Thousands of frigate birds sailed and circled and dove in high flight, without the slightest motion of their wings, and large flocks of booby birds worked out to sea on their daily quest of food. Life and strife were manifest everywhere.

I baited my heavy tackle and trolled. For a minute only I trolled. A jack crevalle seized my bait, and as he tore off with it frigate birds swooped down to see what I had stirred up. Before I could pull the crevalle in a large shark grabbed him and fled, and also took part of my line.

Great numbers of fish were feeding. I noticed a commotion on the water far out. Birds screamed and darted there, and repeatedly large fish broke through, smashing and pounding. I started toward the spot, but was promptly halted by a very hard strike. Away went the fish on a long hard run. I did not have much mercy on him, knowing if I did not get him quickly I would not get him at all. I won by a very narrow margin. Many big brown sharks, hot on his trail, showed up at the moment of gaffing. This catch was a yellow-fin tuna of about sixty pounds.

There was a surprising number of tuna and sharks visible underwater, and I observed that so long as the tuna were not maimed or bloody they could move unmolested among the vicious scavengers.

A moment later I hooked another tuna. The sharks took after him, and then my troubles began. I landed only half of him. The blood in his trail excited the near-by sharks, and their antics brought others, and soon the ocean seemed alive with them. I did not feel any too good in my little boat surrounded by these wolves of the sea.

I yelled to Z. G. and Romer, who were in another boat, to come my way. "Schools of yellow fin!" I shouted. "Big ones!"

I was in the midst of action and sound. Booby birds beat about and added their peculiar cries.

Before the other boat could reach me a big tuna hit Romer's plug and disappeared in a large patch of foam. Romer yelled and hung on, but the fish tore the hook out. We were literally riding on tuna. I saw some that looked all of 300 pounds. Scores of smaller ones, from fifty to a hundred pounds, were chasing bait fish through the water, and above them swooped the birds, making frantic efforts to get their share. Big sharks plowed past them, monsters fifteen and twenty feet in length.

Again Romer had a terrific strike, and almost simultaneously Z. G.'s bait was snatched. Both hooked their fish. Then my attention was diverted by a strike of my own. Driven by sharks, this fish ran like a scared deer. I threw off the drag, giving him a free line. He circled and came back to the boat, and meanwhile I wound and pulled without let-up. Soon came the inevitable jerk of a shark. I hauled hard and made the boatman grab the leader and tug, too. But our struggle was in vain. There was a tremendous splash. Fins and tail showed above the water, and then the head of the tuna appeared, followed by the broad flat head of a shark with the remainder of the tuna in his mouth. He bit the body clear, leaving the head dangling to my hook. Other sharks were fighting furiously for that right at the boatside. I waved the head above the water. A frightful commotion followed. The sharks actually charged the boat, some reaching out of the water in their frenzy to win. Dozens of hungry ferocious-looking devils were just under us. Bob jabbed a big spear into their heads as they came within reach. The smell of blood drove them wild. They tore their wounded mates to pieces or followed after their red trails. Frankly, I did not enjoy the situation.

I looked for the other boat. They were having a battle royal. Romer was trying to save a tuna. His dad was standing up, gun in hand, pumping .30 government shells at the sharks and evidently enjoying it, since at each shot he let out a lusty yell. We saved three small tuna out of the scramble. All the big fish we hooked either broke away or were eaten by the sharks.

How terrible the unremitting strife of the sea! During the days we spent at the Cocos Islands we were ever aware of it, and saw in this fastness of nature's that indeed only the fit could survive.

ROMER'S BIG WAHOO

DOLPHIN OFF THE GALAPAGOS

CHAPTER IX

ANGLING IN THE GALAPAGOS ARCHIPELAGO

PERHAPS the person most reluctant to leave the Cocos Islands and set sail for the Galapagos was my nephew, Romer. I think at the Cocos, where he had a light-tackle orgy, he really overfished his dad and me. The innocence he could assume after smuggling to his boat no end of perishable paraphernalia was great to behold.

I cannot remember the astonishing number of artificial baits he lost, but he did manage to hold some of the large fish; and when he would get one to the boat, he would laugh at us in high glee. Besides landing a record wahoo of fifty pounds, he caught the largest game fish of our Cocos Island visit, a tuna of 155 pounds— that, however, on standard tackle. Romer was of the mind that one good fishing-ground was worth a dozen yet to be explored; so the creak of the lifting anchor had no music for him, and departure only regret, until the spirit for adventure reawakened.

Once more we were headed south. We traveled at a fair rate of speed. The ocean was calm, with enough of a breeze to fill the sails and help us along. We were nearing the equator, yet the weather was pleasant, warm but not uncomfortable. We saw very few signs of fish the first two days, although the tropical sea was at its best.

Then came a night when I was awakened by a rush of wind bellying the sails, and going on deck I found it dark as pitch. A heavy storm had suddenly come upon us and was driving the ship before it. The wind roared, the sails flapped, booms creaked, and the rain came down in torrents. The air was fragrant with a familiar scent of spring showers. The storm passed as suddenly as it had come, and soon we were riding through moon- and star-light.

As we neared the Galapagos Islands we noticed a marked drop in temperature. The air was spiced and invigorating. This change was due to the Humbolt current, a stream of cold water which flows off the coast of South America and passes the Galapagos Islands. It is similar to the Gulf Stream in the Atlantic, which runs along the eastern coast of the United States; but the former is of cold water, and the latter warm.

From here on, small fish were in sight most of the time, also schools of tuna, porpoise, and dolphin. One afternoon we were watching a school of tuna and dolphin feeding upon small fish. Doubling their energies for our benefit, they jumped and played and dove, and crossed and recrossed our vessel's bow. Tuna and porpoise in the air at once! What delight! This dolphin was not the beautiful leaping creature of the Atlantic, but similar to the porpoise, except that he excelled him in size.

We were treated to warm summer squalls, and as I watched the several deluges of rain I was envious for California, where skies are less generous.

On the fourth day we sighted Pinta Island, the first of the Galapagos group. A speck on the horizon it lay, but what a sight for landlubbers! Under a speed of nine knots an hour and covering about that distance, we came in line with Marchina. It was barren, desolate, a toneless gray; yet it fascinated us. What a contrast to the tropical Cocos Islands!

We were a thousand miles from Panama and getting well in sight of the whole of the Galapagos group. At five minutes after one, on the afternoon of February

10th, we passed over the equator. We celebrated this occasion with the ringing of bells and blowing of whistles. In my mind, the equator was always associated with tremendous heat, but that association was dispelled, for a fine cool breeze blew, making the temperature delightful.

Isabella Island, Albemarle, and then Santa Cruz, generally called Indefatigable, the largest island of the group, appeared in the distance. Presently we were attracted by great splashes in the water ahead of us, which proved to be made by leaping giant rays. Some were fifteen feet across the back, others twenty-five, black in color, with white undersides. They created an amazing sight when they made complete turns in the air.

Z. G. remarked upon the scarcity of bird life. We had seen only a few birds, and they were new and strange. One was almost pure white with a tail of two long slender feathers, about eight inches in length. Swift and graceful, these birds gave gladsome relief to the monotony of the lonely ocean. A solitary small tern, very delicate and dainty, with jet-black body and little white tail, followed us, seemingly pleased with our company.

Indefatigable, where we were to seek harbor, rose gently from the sea to a lofty central peak around which dark storm clouds were formed, letting down gray shafts of rain. Soon the contour and color of the place became more defined; slopes showed bleak and rugged, and tones of red and slate and silver and melting yellow gave a desert atmosphere. It was majestic, lonely, barren, unclaimed. Late in the afternoon we anchored in Harrison Cove, Conway Bay, a good anchorage with smooth, peaceful water.

Romer, our champion go-getter, immediately put a line overboard and before long hauled up a four-foot sand shark. The water swarmed with like beggars that missed out in the fight to reach the ship. Below them small fish, gold gleaming on black, went maneuvering quietly about, untempted and serene.

Conway Bay typified peaceful desolation, a desert of land meeting a desert of sea. Slowly moving green swells broke into sheets of white water as they washed the rock-bound glistening beach before us.

The sun faded behind Eden Island and Albemarle, playing great shafts of silver light high in the heavens, and suddenly evening settled down upon us. Then clouds of mosquitoes came offshore, a silent host that foraged off our hides and became drunk with the rare vintage of human blood, until complete darkness of night somehow drove them into obscurity. Then we had peace, complete peace—an almost too enduring silence. There was no sound of insect, bird, or beast. The Galapagos Islands were indeed, as Beebe called them, "World's End."

Early in the morning we hastened to go ashore. A seal, unafraid and curious, swam alongside our boat clear to the shallow water, where with lazy satisfaction he at last abandoned us.

The sun shone hot on the wide white shore. Mosquitoes rediscovered us and shared us with sand flies. Beyond the stretch of beach was impenetrable thorny brush and cactus, and beyond that fortification black beds of lava rock gave hold to a sparsely scattered growth. When we skirted the shore, sharp lava rock cut into our shoes, making progress most difficult and unpleasant. Our efforts to break through the jungle of thorns made us appreciate why Indefatigable had never been explored.

Romer was inspired to investigate everything that came to his notice in this intriguing place. It flamed his imagination little less than it did his father's. He was soon on the trail of strange tracks in the sand, broad tracks with decorative flourishes made by long curved claws. They led to jagged rocks along the water's edge, where a four-foot lizard, ferocious of mien, lay sunning himself. He was the color of lava, had rough scaly hide and a long tail, and in all was much like the desert gila monster, though a giant by comparison of size.

This was the famed marine iguana of Indefatigable, almost extinct now, a gentle harmless creature despite his formidable appearance. We trailed numbers of them. They clung so tenaciously to the rocks, aided by sharp claws and great strength of legs, that we found it difficult to lift them free. We coralled several, and later, when we released them, we bet on which would reach the water first, and thereby inaugurated iguana races which made keen sport for the boys.

In all the pools left by the receding tides were tiny fish, gems of color—gold, green, purple, indigo, and black—lithe, swift creatures that usually outwitted our artful attempts to catch them. Crabs were present in abundance. All the sea-washed rocks had these brilliant fire-red crustaceans shifting to and fro over them.

Unable to resist the urge to fish, we put out in our launches for two of the smaller islands, Guy Fawke and Seymour. Green turtles were plentiful but wary, ducking under the sunny surface of the water when we came close. Around Guy Fawke Island we found seals and iguanas affably sharing the choicest rock sites. The iguanas had no fear of us while we kept our distance, but the seals barked impolitely.

A lonely booby caught my attention. He was diving for fish from a high perch, spotting his prey with remarkable keenness and darting to capture it with rocket-like speed. He never made a miss. We intended to compete with Mr. Booby from our three launches, but had no assurance that we would enjoy such success. Action, however, proved fast and furious.

As soon as we put our lines over, small tuna, which were present in great numbers and obviously hungry, dove for our baits. They were of the yellow-fin variety, hard-fighting little fellows weighing from forty to sixty pounds. We had high hopes for the fishing possibilities and were on the lookout for swordfish and sailfish. Two large hammerhead sharks fooled me for a while into thinking they were swordfish.

An immense school of ballyhoo came into the air just ahead of me, shining like a silver cloud. They skidded over the water with a violent precipitation that left no doubt they were being pursued by larger game. The ballyhoo with which I was familiar were very small compared with these. There was no lack of excitement— not a minute's lull in fishing. I watched the other boats. Both Z. G. and Romer were busy as net fishermen after a haul. Romer, in particular, did not let up for a moment. He made every motion count. We caught many tuna, small dolphin, grouper, rock-hind, and cero-mackerel. The cero-mackerel ran very large, about fifteen pounds, exceeding in size by several pounds any we had ever taken elsewhere.

On my way back to the ship I was thrilled by a smashing strike and wonderfully fast run. After a brief, invigorating struggle, I had to my credit a forty-five pound wahoo, a record in my own achievements.

I could not convey news of my good fortune to the other boats because they had become involved in action themselves. I saw a beautiful dolphin leap frantically in outward gesture from Z. G.'s boat, saw Romer tearing to the scene and heard my name in hurried command to rush on with the cameras. The dolphin leaped repeatedly in a glorious blaze of color.

Romer and I mouthed all kinds of directions on how to land the fish, recommending especially that Z. G.

MARINE IGUANAS, GALAPAGOS. THESE LIZARDS ARE FOUR FEET LONG, FEROCIOUS-LOOKING, BUT QUITE HARMLESS

MOTHER FASCINATED AND BABY SCARED

play him hard and fast to avoid the pursuit of sharks, but we were squelched with the suggestion that we tend to the cameras and leave the fishing to him. We did, and presently Zane, coming through the victor, roared his joy at us. It was an exceptional specimen in form and color, and it weighed fifty pounds—another high-mark in our experience.

Day after day, under a blistering sun, we ran the ocean, searching for big game. None showed, but around the neighboring islands and close along the shore of Indefatigable the water was alive with small fish. The scarcity of the large species was a disappointment to us, but we contented ourselves with the excitement of being hooked on, without cessation, to surprisingly numerous varieties of the lesser kind. It was a paradise for a fisherman, action every minute, and some of it strenuous enough to test the skill of a veteran.

A needlefish, some three feet long, resenting the indignity of capture, took it upon himself to bite my boatman, and stirred considerable excitement and mirth. The needlefish has very large jaws and sharp long teeth, and this one, being in an aggressive mood, was to be respected. With a sinuous motion he made for the nearest enemy and closed down on his leg. Yells, exclamations (deleted by the censor), and a noisy scramble followed. The boatman slammed the fish on the bottom of the boat and stamped on him. We saw blood stains on his trousers where the fish had taken hold. Biting fish were new to us. We exercised more care in handling the next one.

At noon each day the sun burned down with terrific heat; then heavy, dull-gray storm clouds would form over Indefatigable and rain fall in torrents. Sometimes these showers would cool the atmosphere, but usually they were too far away.

One morning Romer and I undertook a little fishing trip of our own. It was cloudy most of the time, with a comfortable cool breeze, and we had one short shower. We enjoyed the company of small black gulls of an alien breed that fed unceasingly on the schools of small fish. They were the first birds we had seen in any considerable numbers since our arrival at these strange, silent islands of the Pacific. The moment we put baits over, small tuna were after them. Immediately Romer's rod was bobbing up and down and some unlucky fish was running hard to leeward. There was no overtaking that kind of a fish; you gave him his head and let him run. The tuna fought hard. Romer perspired freely, but enjoyed it none the less. We caught seven tuna averaging thirty pounds each, and between the catches Romer never ceased to ejaculate on the joy of it.

"Some fishing, Uncle Rome! I like this! No waiting for bites! Now watch this next one!"

We congratulated ourselves on the absence of sharks, but when with mighty splash a big brown body darted after a large mackerel which Romer was working and tore it from his hook, we were jolted out of that delusion. We had been approaching a small island which seemed a likely place for fishing. The waves rolled high upon its sides and battered their strength there. A giant ray jumped ahead of us, and then another. We tried for photographs. Later I had a tremendous strike. The fish made a running leap through the air and shook himself free, but not before we all had a good look at a very large tuna.

Another terrible strike followed. As was the case nine times out of ten you had no idea what took your bait. Romer declared this was a tuna, and a whale of a one. I saw nothing. The fish felt very heavy, so I was assured he at least was large. After a back-breaking fight I pulled him up to where we could reach the leader. My first glimpse of him, deep in the water, fooled me, but my second glance gave me the truth. It was a shark. We soon assassinated him. One grows to hate big sharks. There are so many, and they always turn up when fishing looks best.

This was the first of a number of shark fights. They came, larger and larger, and presently sharks twenty feet in length surrounded us. Romer gloried in it, but the absence of the other boats made me a little nervous. Our launch seemed to shrink in size in the presence of these fighting devils. In this instance wisdom was the better part of valor, wherefore I insisted we leave that locality.

We turned back and were soon among a congregation of giant rays. Romer wanted a try at one; so we rigged up a small iron we had on board, tied it to a quarter-inch rope and were then ready to court trouble. The lad missed his mark on the first ray he tackled; but there was another near by, and he quickly jabbed the iron into him. We certainly had taken on a hair-raising job! Of all the diving, sousing, splashing, and scurrying for freedom, and dogged determination to drag us out to sea!

The ray towed us at his pleasure but not without resistance on the part of our engineer and boatman. We spent most of the afternoon trying to subdue him, and it took four of us at that. While I was completely exhausted, Romer was in his glory—his clothes were torn, his hands were cut, yet he stuck to that ray like a leech. We licked the monster, but I made a resolution right then and there never to tackle another one, which resolution I have faithfully kept. This ray measured fifteen feet across the back and weighed fifteen hundred pounds.

On the way back to the *Fisherman* we met one of the other boats coming in search of us. Z. G. had grown anxious when evening approached and we had not yet appeared, so had put out in our direction.

The fight with the ray was my most exciting experience during our stay off Indefatigable. In the following days we fished around the several islands and caught many different varieties of small fish and some fine wahoo, and found tuna, rays, and sharks most plentiful, but we saw no sign whatever of either sailfish or swordfish.

We sailed from Indefatigable to Tower Island, sixty-five miles northeast, on a beautiful sea ruffled by a breeze that made the journey very pleasant for us. *En route* we saw dolphin, rays, and several small whales. Many years ago Charles Darwin visited Tower Island. Today its one bay bears his name—a bay formed in the partly sunken crater of an extinct volcano where a high semicircular wall, grim and formidable, stops the sea.

I sat on the ship's deck that evening in the delicate coolness of a perfect tropical night, feeling a strange depression because of the terrible loneliness of that forsaken place. The island seemed like a prison fortress. I remembered that Spaniards had called the place Nightmare Island. How felicitously named!

In the morning sunlight Darwin Bay took on a more cheerful aspect. We were anchored in water smooth as crystal and as clear. Schools of bright-colored fish swam back and forth under the boat, and all around were hammerhead sharks lazily sunning themselves on the surface.

From the side of the ship Romer caught several trigger fish, grouper, and strange gold-and-gray fish, and then took to shooting at the sharks with a big rifle. "I sure love to kill them off!" he confided to me, with an emphasis behind which was memory of all too many game fish brought to gaff bodyless.

Tower Island was the home of thousands of frigate

and booby birds, and doves and gulls, nesting together indiscriminately. They were very tame; they showed no fear whatever when we picked them up. We found baby boobies white as snow and soft as thistle-down, and the young of other species in various homely stages of growth. Black and white gulls walked near us inquiringly, uttering plaintive calls, and one lonesome dove, who seemed lost among the larger birds, dogged my heels until I made an attempt to coax him to my hand. Directly overhead the sky was black with birds. They circled high and low, bickering, scolding, chattering endlessly. When we left them a sea-lion, who resented our visit, chased us to our boats.

We ran outside the bay in our little launch and found the surf pounding on the shore. Great sharks were riding the swells, while above us thousands of little black swallows with white-rimmed tails enjoyed their elements whole-heartedly. The sharks traveled in schools, which to us was most surprising. They were long bodied and had black-tipped fins.

Off Tower Island we had no lack of wonderful, exciting fishing. There were finds for us there. Beautiful golden fish large as sea bass showed, and long shiny green fish struck at our baits. As fast as we would drop a bait into the water some fish would take it; and as fast as we would hook a fish, a shark would tear it from us. A grouper of forty pounds made one neat bite for a hungry shark. We worked and persevered, but it was of no use. The miserable scavengers were too much for us.

Eventually we ran around to the windward side of the island. Here Romer, after violent efforts, got a large wahoo near the boat, only to see it cut in two by the savage rush of a big black shark. Later I pulled up the head of a large tuna. It had been severed from the body at the gills.

Z. G., in another boat, was having his troubles, too. Driven to desperation, we organized to go after the sharks in earnest. We took them on with our heaviest tackle, guns, and lances. I never saw my brother work so violently. He would pull a 500-pound shark to the boat in remarkably short time, and then carnage would follow. With our pestilent enemy shot and lanced, the commotion on the water was awful. Some shark, this black terror!

Romer and I rotated action from our boat. I would try to recover while he had a go. I broke my lines, broke my good rod, and almost broke my back. Sharks? Shades of Father Neptune they were thick! We fought them savagely; and they, meanwhile, maddened by the scent of blood, flocked around us and battled with one another.

I watched Z. G., active under a relentless sun, trying to steady his movements in a bobbing little boat. I was worried every minute, and glad when a ferocious, aggressive shark chewed his wire leader in two and made him pause long enough to reflect on the folly of continuing the shambles longer.

We returned to the *Fisherman* in a demoralized condition. Our experience at the Cocos Islands had been heroic enough, but this had been appalling. May I never encounter this same species of shark again!

That night I was awakened by a rolling of the *Fisherman*. She groaned and pulled at her anchor chains. Hurriedly I dressed and went on deck to find a howling wind blowing and solid sheets of rain washing over the ship. The night was black—so black you could not see your hand before you. I had misgivings as I thought of the lonely forbidding island, and the deep black crater where we rode. It we were washed ashore on Nightmare Island, it would be a tragic ending of the voyage of the *Fisherman*.

ANGLING IN THE GALAPAGOS ARCHIPELAGO

But the wind seemed to be coming offshore; though the ship dragged at her anchor, she drifted in the right direction. After half an hour of violence the rain stopped and the wind subsided as quickly as it had come. Such seemed always to be the case in these southerly storms.

We sailed toward the north in the morning, leaving the black desolation of this last place on earth. The memory of the stark loneliness, the fierce black sharks, and the shrill, mournful cries of the millions of birds will always remain with me. The Galapagos Archipelago had afforded us wonderful fishing and exciting, thrilling adventures, but I felt relieved when Indefatigable, Albemarle, and the outlying islands faded in the distance and again we were following the wide pastures of the sea.

CHAPTER X

RICH WATERS OF ZIHUATANEJO

TWO weeks sailing north on pleasing smooth seas carried us far from Panama, midway up the coast of old Mexico. At daylight one morning, in the early part of March, we lay outside the town of Zihuatanejo, where a solitary rock, forty feet high, marked the entrance to the narrow opening to the bay, waiting for favorable conditions to run in. It was along these shores we had imagined we would find extraordinary fishing and hunting.

A great and rugged mountain range rose above the bay. The sea had encroached upon a span of low land and there formed a perfect sheltered harbor. The water was calm as a lake. It lapped the wide white beach lazily. A grove of tall slender coconut trees lined the shore and on the side hills shone the broad green leaves of the banana trees. When we passed into the bay a flock of yellow-headed parrots flew from their nesting-places to screech at us.

At the farthest corner of the bay was the little village of Zihuatanejo, which we found to be most primitive and sleepy, and lost from civilization. Some houses were made of adobe, others of palm thatch. All were low in structure. They ran in color from delicate pink to muddy yellow, from bright green of fresh palm fronds to seared ocher of faded ones.

The streets, short avenues from a main broad plaza, were soft with deep sand. Wide and low-spreading branches of old gnarled trees shaded the village from the hot rays of the sun. Everywhere children played,

End of the Fight

NOTE THE HUGE SAIL

Coming Out Upside Down

SAILFISH

and with them, family fashion, were dogs, chickens, and pigs. Two diminutive deer pattered fearlessly in and out one group. Women cooked over small fires, while men, clad in white shirts and trousers of many a cut and color, stood idly by.

Cross-breeds of Spaniards, Mexicans, and Indians, with a few pure types, made up the population. The strain of Spanish blood carried down from the days when Cortez and his men landed on the shore of this inviting bay. We saw several strikingly beautiful children with black hair and eyes familiar to old Spain. They were haughty and aloof, not eager and vivacious as were other children of their age.

So remote was the village from cultural influences that it had continued for centuries in much the same primitive state in which Cortez had found it. There were no churches or schools, and children knew no such things as toys. They gathered playthings from the family live-stock.

The natives recognized our photographs of Marlin and broadbill swordfish. They also described another great leaping fish in terms so concise that they left no doubt that they referred to sailfish. They declared that earlier in the year these different kinds of fish, predominantly the sailfish, passed the bay in great numbers on their way south. There was promise of good fortune here, and we lost no time setting about to investigate it.

Our first day of fishing was full of thrills. Excitement prevailed as soon as we left the bay and found ourselves in a school of leaping dolphin. They cut the water every-where. Beyond, several whales were blowing. As soon as I sighted them I signaled Z. G. and we turned their way. Such active blowing and diving! As we drew close we found they were sperm whales. They sounded, but had the good grace to return to the surface and give us splendid opportunities for photographs. One whale brought yells of delight when he exhibited a great white tail, something we had never before been privileged to see.

Z. G. and Romer risked their lives to get good pictures. In the fascination of the chase we all ran too close to the sounding area, but danger was forgotten through those thrilling moments. The whales threw spouts of spray fifteen feet in the air, making a peculiar whistling sound with each expulsion.

One of the black-tailed whales kept close by the white-tailed fellow. At times they sounded together, and their great broad tails, lifted high, showed in spectacular contrast. There was an unparalleled magnificence in the sight. We could not leave them while they played so enticingly. First would come white spray of the breaking water, then the heaving motion of the tremendous back as it appeared, a great forward movement leading down, hardly permitting the full body to show, then the tail alone, vertical in the air, a great flashing fan that soon disappeared. We ran south to the White Friars, the cluster of twelve islands that had so intrigued us from aboard the steamer when we were bound for Panama. They rose from one to two hundred feet above water, and were white with guano accumulation of many years. At sight of us clouds of birds filled the air to circle high and scream defiance. Their aerie was indeed cosmopolitan, for with thousands of boobies were many white jaegers with long streaming tails, and strange black birds resembling small gulls.

The water around these islands was as full of fish as the air was full of birds. Never had we seen so many hungry fish or had so many strikes. The slightest motion of baits on the water started combat. The fish flopped over one another in their efforts to reach the baits, hard-fighting crevalle of forty pounds, enormous red snappers

of sixty pounds and more, yellowtail twice the size of
any I had ever seen at Catalina, mackerel of fifteen
pounds, big rooster-fish and needlefish three and four
feet long. It seemed that throughout the journey on these
southern seas we moved from one peak of activity to
another, each place surpassing the last.

I saw Z. G. hook a very heavy rooster-fish. It was a
high and lofty tumbler, a most terrific fighter. He kept
the air astir with silver flashes. This was the beginning
of many thrilling sessions with rooster-fish. Some measured five feet in length and ran to seventy-five pounds
in weight. They were light-tackle busters with a
vengeance.

Around the White Friars the water was free from
sharks, and we fished undisturbed and to our hearts' content. On our return to the ship I saw three sailfish jumping, Z. G. had a broadbill hooked for a few minutes,
and Romer became engaged with a large Marlin which,
after jumping four times, broke the line. By this time
our excitement was so intense that fishing caution was
abandoned. We cared little if the fish were too large
for our tackle—come one come all—for this was a time
when our fishing appetites were satisfied.

Every day the sea was smooth and blue, making generously comfortable fishing water, and light trade winds
gave us delightful summer weather. There were so many
places to go and so much to do that we wondered how
we could make time for them all.

One day Romer and I ran up the coast to a wide, high
beach, above which showed green trees that fringed a
lagoon. A trip up the lagoon in a small rowboat opened
our eyes to the hunting possibilities of the country. We
saw many small deer and quantities of birds—pelicans
and white cranes, ducks and geese, snipe, plover, cor-
morants and curlew. What a haven for game birds! Here

I had my first sight of the beautiful pink flamingoes traveling in a large flock.

On our way back to the *Fisherman* we ran around the White Friars, which were too temptingly near for us to neglect. Always our approach startled many birds to flight. Since we had not molested them, we preferred to think that this procedure was purely their way of greeting us. If they had any fear, it left them as soon as we put baits overboard. They then made nuisances of themselves, diving for the baits so assiduously that rarely did a fish get a chance at them. But fish were there and we enjoyed watching them.

When we left the Friars we ran into a stiff westerly wind that whipped the sea into big white-caps and sent spray over us, wetting us thoroughly.

One of our choice places for baits we felicitously named Black Rock. There, one morning, I passed a big sailfish swimming on the surface. He was traveling along fast, as if in search of food. I circled him and let out a bait where he could see it plainly. He made a running dive and took the bait from my hook as clean as any kingfish had ever done. Nothing finicky about that fish! He meant business and hit my bait like a Marlin swordfish.

Another sailfish jumped in the distance. Time after time he slashed the water. Forthwith I hailed the other boat and told Z. G. and Romer my hard-luck story and started them with me on a race to find the last fish.

Still another jumped a short distance from Z. G.'s boat. Presently I saw a blue fin sail up to Romer's artificial bait, and there followed a savage yank as a long fish grabbed it. Greatly excited, Romer bungled his strike, and then out into the air came a heavy sailfish, which, with a mighty shake, threw the plug twenty feet high. Z. G. called the boy pretty severely for not striking harder, but in the excitement I think he forgot it would be very difficult to hook a sailfish on a plug.

Several more sailfish showed—long, powerful jumpers. I watched my bait carefully. Two catastrophes were sufficient. It was going to fall to the lot of one of us to catch the first Pacific sailfish. About noon, after patient fishing, I saw a purple-and-brown streak coming for my bait. I was all ready, and as he took the bait, turning rapidly with it, I set the hook with three good husky yanks. Thus the fray started.

The sailfish sent water flying everywhere. He was long, big around, and black. Down he would go, and then rise to leap frantically. Cameras clicked. I could hear Romer yelling advice. What fisherman can resist fighting another man's fish in this manner, begging him to all kinds of caution? The thrill of Long Key fishing days returned, enhanced by the knowledge of a master specimen on hand.

Fifteen wonderful jumps he made in his efforts to get away. He was a great fighter. Even at the boat he drenched us all while we were tying him up. But as I looked at him I felt rewarded. Z. G. loves a sailfish, and commenting on this one he was profuse in his praise of its beauty and force as a fighter. It was nine feet four and a half inches in length and ran well over 100 pounds. He differed in points from the Atlantic sailfish. He was very dark and glossy, with deep purple stripes showing on his sides, and had a very broad and powerful tail and a broad sail, purple and blue, with black spots.

My luck inspired the others. Sailfishing became the order of the day. It was not long before Z. G. attracted our attention to a sail moving high above water behind his bait. What thrilling adventure! I saw the fish hit the bait, take it quickly, and disappear. Z. G. made a clean miss, at which Romer winked somberly at me.

Fishing was much at a standstill after that. I had another thrill when a whopper of a Marlin, which would surely have gone over 500 pounds, followed my bait. He stayed deep and watched the bait distrustfully for a while. In the end he decided he had no use for it. This was an auspicious day for me and boded well for future events.

At sundown near Black Rock I watched Romer catch a sixty-pound red snapper and battle with four husky rooster-fish. That night we were possessed with the subject of sailfish and Marlin, and planned astounding victories.

About five miles above Zihuatanejo Bay were the Moro Rocks, another aerie, but one which belonged to parrots and macaws. Their numbers were legion and their general protest whenever we arrived resounded in a clamor and excitement heretofore unparalleled. Perhaps it was nesting season and they were afraid we would disturb their young. At any rate, it was unique to be screamed at so shrilly and unbrokenly while pursuing an innocent pleasure.

Heavy currents and channels passed between the islands, and here we had scores of feverish successful fights with the rooster-fish. They were powerful, fast, and possessed almost endless endurance. Many would run the whole length of the islands, two or three hundred yards. Fishing resolved into wild races through boiling water. Much light tackle was smashed at this place, proof of enjoyable hours.

The screaming and calling of the macaws still ring in my ears. Long will I remember the quantities of fish, the great joy and strenuous action Z. G. found at Moro Rocks, and the wonderful ever-evident enthusiasm of Romer. Never had a young boy been so busy or had so many brilliant combats with so many varieties of fish.

Z. G. and Romer had a contest for the largest rooster-fish. As I recall, Z. G. won out in the end, although it took a mighty big one to beat Romer's.

Days passed quickly. We lost track of time. From early morning to sunset we were busily running the sea. If we tired of hunting sailfish, a short run to some of the rocks along the shore would afford immediate results among giant snappers, amberjacks, crevalle, or rooster-fish. It was no trouble to get the anglers out in the morning. They were up at peep of dawn, making elaborate preparation, mending tackle, testing lines, gathering everything necessary for a successful venture, and as my old cowboy used to say, "r'arin' to go."

Following our first experience with sailfish, Romer and I had a bad day together. I precipitated misfortune by losing the first sailfish we saw on its maiden jump. After that great sailfish appeared behind the baits, refused to take them or struck at them in blind fashion, or took them too gingerly. Romer missed three sailfish in succession, and I, not up to form myself, let two beggars, whose terrific strikes yanked my arms sore, make a neat escape.

But this was Z. G.'s lucky day. While we were having our troubles he was enjoying himself hooking a fine sail-fish, getting many beautiful jumps from it and joking us about our poor fishing.

To add to our distress, Romer hooked a big hammer-head shark, which delayed further sailfishing for a while. I sat in the shade of a big umbrella and watched the stubborn fight. Romer worked vigorously, mindless of a hot sun, although he looked at times as if he might break under the strain. He proved unyielding. A 400-pound hammerhead is really a man's job, but Romer finished this old scavenger in less time than I could have done it.

A little later, when we were close on Z. G.'s track, we

saw him jump hurriedly from the seat and point behind the boat where the wake of a fish and then a small black fin appeared. As quickly as the fin showed it disappeared, and it must have been at that moment that the fish took the bait. Z. G. struck savagely three times, and then the sea opened and out came the most wonderful Marlin swordfish we had ever seen. It must have weighed 500 pounds—that at least. Sight of him was a breath-taking spectacle. Romer and I rushed for our cameras.

My heart sank as I remembered that Z. G. was using light tackle. I had stuck to my heavy tackle, expecting this very thing to happen, but Z. G. had gone back to a light outfit, keeping a heavy one baited at his side. Such was the irony of fate. I looked up to see the magnificent fish upright, shooting over the water on his tail.

He was heavier than my first calculation allowed. We were dumfounded, almost paralyzed to inaction.

Z. G. was the most dazed of any of us. He stood up. His grip on his rod was viselike as his eyes followed that lordly fish. Again the Marlin straightened out and started away on a long run, jumping as he ran. We turned in pursuit. Romer for once was quiet, and I knew he felt the tragedy of this encounter. Z. G. stood only one chance in a hundred of catching that fish on light tackle.

I was sick because catastrophe seemed imminent. This was the greatest Marlin we had ever looked upon— shoulders all of three feet, a thick powerful body and, oh, what a tail!

Z. G. settled down to the greatest battle of his life. He had nothing to say; he seemed overcome by the hopelessness of the task before him. We watched the great fight of our time. Four hours Z. G. with delicate deftness and skill battled with the fish in the wan hope of mastering him. We followed them miles out, and we photo-

R. C. Grey with Particularly Wonderful Specimen of Sailfish

THREE SAILFISH TAKEN IN ONE DAY

graphed and shouted praises whenever Z. G. got the least advantage.

In the last hour he had the double line on the reel time and again, but because the final lifting could not be achieved, he repeatedly lost long footage to the Marlin. We could only guess what transpired in his boat. We knew there was intense excitement on board and grim determination in Z. G.'s work. We saw the boatman get the leader in his hands time after time, but fail to lift the fish. I nearly expired while watching this.

Finally, after an almost superhuman effort on Z. G.'s part to regain the line and get the leader, the double line parted! Z. G. slumped down exhausted. Afterward he told me that he felt he would never get over the exasperating, horrible, inevitable nature of that catastrophe.

It was a sad and forlorn return we made to the *Fisherman*. Z. G. was in bad shape for a couple of days, so we eased up on the fishing.

Throughout our stay at Zihuatanejo we had numerous visits from the natives. Whole families would come, and always in gala dress. Time meant so little to these people that all their visits were overlong. They were curious about the motor-boats, so what time one was available we sent parties out in relays to enjoy a spin.

When we renewed our fishing we went in quest of broadbill, and for three days roamed the sea from Moro Rocks to White Friars. There were none to be found, but the boats sighted numerous sailfish, had a number of strikes, and in all three catches. Z. G.'s enthusiasm returned. This was again the most wonderful place in all the world, with the most perfect fishing conditions.

Another never-to-be-forgotten day Z. G. fought a powerful sailfish, while Romer took what proved to be some of our finest photographs. The fish gave every opportunity for them. He leaped time and time again. We counted and called louder with each successive leap. He leaped close at hand, and he leaped far away, on which sprints he had us tearing after him. He inspired us with his beauty, yet his size made him seem unattainable.

Carefully as Z. G. worked, there were moments when the fish on his far-away runs might easily have escaped. But in the end an outspread sail moved weakly toward the boat, and a spent sailfish surrendered to the gaff. Romer shouted: "Forty-three clear jumps! Some fish! A beauty for light tackle. Gee! you gave a wonderful exhibition, Dad. Maybe I can repeat that on my light tackle."

It was the largest sailfish we had ever seen—a beautiful record fish measuring ten feet one inch and weighing 135 pounds.

Although we met with a number of rebuffs in the days that followed, our fishing ardor did not cool. We lost some chances of getting big Marlin and lost some sailfish.

Romer began to feel that he was not slated to catch a sailfish because of his inexperience at this phase of deep-sea sport, but there came a time, eight days after his last sailfish was lost from his hook, when he made a beautiful strike and treated himself to a splendid fight, very active and spectacular on the part of the fish, and exceedingly solemn and deadly on the part of the young man. He fought like a veteran and in half an hour had a tired-out sailfish alongside the boat. He let him run off again for several final slow leaps. Then the hook pulled out. Romer, like a thorough sport, was satisfied.

Z. G. has always claimed that I am a lucky angler. Perhaps I am. At any rate, many great fishing experiences have fallen to my lot and culminated in a wonderful way. Just such a remarkable run of events topped this fishing trip for me, and it all began off Black Rock, where I had made my start for the day. It was one of those times of almost instant action.

First I hooked a sailfish that bested me by throwing the hook. Then it was only a little while until another long purple fin showed behind my bait. It is hard to admit that I missed this fish four times, my line meantime paying farther and farther out. When I made an effective strike, the fish must have been five hundred feet from the boat. Then my troubles began; and no joke about that! Leap after leap took more line, and we ran after him in desperation.

The fish cut the water clear fifty-three times and practically exhausted himself with his exhibition. I was elated. Soon after he was hoisted aboard I hooked another. His first leap was at record height. He was a speed fiend. He did not jump much, but he ran and darted all over and put me on my mettle. To our surprise, he came up tail first. Presently the cause was disclosed. The broken leader was hanging from his mouth. The wire had cut through the fin, and the only thing that held the fish was the swivel. By very careful handling I brought him to gaff.

Still my luck continued. After slacking my line and bait back a considerable number of times, I hooked a third fish. I nailed him a good distance from the boat, and he jumped wildly. I had a big bag in the line, and we had to slow up, but the fish did not quit jumping. Suddenly, close to my boat, another sailfish appeared with my line in his mouth. He was trying to bite it in two.

I slacked off the line, and on the instant the fish I was fighting jumped and in some way threw the line around the bill of the newcomer. With a terrible crash the latter came out, turned over, and went down head first. He came out the second time entangled in the line. Here I was tied to two fish at once! Things were happening with appalling speed.

Z. G. and Romer yelled to know what was the matter, but I had no time to explain. I was mightily absorbed. To my chagrin, the hooked fish made a frantic leap and freed himself. The meddler, however, was with me still, hopelessly bound, and presently he wore the brand of the gaff.

"Did you ever see anything to equal that?" I stuttered as Z. G. and Romer came alongside.

"You're an old record-maker," Z. G. conceded, "and the darndest, luckiest fisherman in the world!"

That night I wrote in my fish book:

Sailfish 9 ft. 2 in.—weight 100 lbs.

9 ft. 10 in.—weight 113 lbs.

9 ft. 3 in.—weight 118 lbs.

Whale Sounding. R. C. with the Movie Camera

Romer with the 184-pound Yellowfin (Allison) Tuna

CHAPTER XI

## FISH AND CAPE SAN LUCAS

ON OUR way up the coast from Zihuatanejo, Mexico, we ran into a stiff nor'wester which carried us far off our course. The weather was much cooler than any we had encountered. Big green waves with white-coated tops made our schooner lunge and toss. Many of the ship's company were seasick, and sight of the land of Lower California, whither we were bound, was, for this reason, doubly welcomed.

Desert land, with the dearly familiar cactus and greasewood and the fragrant air, seemed like home after the thousands of miles of travel to strange shores over vast strange seas.

As we approached Cape San Lucas we sighted many schools of tuna, some fish of which were very large. A sailfish jumped for us, and offshore a short distance we saw two whales blowing. Again splendid indications of good fishing-grounds! And again an almost landlocked bay, a calm wide expanse of green water! Steep-sloping beaches of white sand ran to the water's edge, and back from the shore were isolated groups of palm trees. Many market fishing boats were in the bay, and one yacht from Los Angeles.

Our first day's scouting proved great claims for Cape San Lucas. Three fishing launches made a formidable aggregation for unsuspecting fish, but we became a badly disorganized fleet when they demonstrated their tactics. We were not prepared for the terrible onslaught of big tuna that was visited upon us. Many were hooked and lost. We could not judge size at first, but they seemed busters—in fact, they turned out to be first-class tackle-busters, ruining rods, leaders, and lines, and stealing artificial baits.

At the very beginning of the day, Z. G. lost three heavy fellows in succession. This convinced him that the twenty-four-thread line he was using would be of no service here. He changed to a thirty-nine-thread line, and then broke his rod-socket and finally his chair. Every time I looked in his direction he was pulling for dear life on a fish. He brought in eight tuna, the largest of which were 218, 180, and 150 pounds. He told us amazing tales of what he had seen and experienced, and judging from his bedraggled condition he was not exaggerating.

From a small ill-equipped boat, which denied them the practically indispensable fishing chairs, Captain Mitchell and Romer were hooked to tuna at the same time, and fought them with antics both surprising and amusing. They would run the length of the boat, wheel and seesaw, duck under each other's lines, become so entangled that disaster threatened, then come out of their difficulties grinning and panting, only to find themselves involved in new ones.

Captain Mitchell smashed his rod, but hung on and succeeded in getting his tuna. Romer was a joy to see. They went on their way, and I learned afterward they broke two more tackles but landed five tuna between them, all averaging 140 pounds.

My attention was attracted to a market fishing-boat near by. I ran close and watched the crew haul in tuna with a speed that left me gasping. Four men stood in the stern of the boat. Three were equipped with stiff bamboo rods, with three-foot·wires substituting for lines and a good-sized hook apiece. The fourth man had a big gaff hook on a short rope. Above them was stationed still another man, who threw out handfuls of small fish from a bait box.

The water beneath the boat was alive with tuna, stampeding in their efforts to get the minnows. A man on the rod, baiting his hook with one of the small fish, would reach out and literally drop the bait into a tuna's mouth; then he would set the hook with a yank and hang on. The man with the gaff hook would reach over, gaff the fish, and forthwith everybody would take the rope and the next second disappear in a deluge of water raised by the tuna in his struggle to get away. They made short work of catches, which were so many that the men had no time to rest—wonderful big tuna, running as large as 300 pounds. Many would escape after being gaffed— easy meals for the hovering sharks.

The market demand on the supply of tuna is great, and I sometimes wonder if, contrary to reports and evasions, they are not decreasing in abundance. Pondering on that very question, I went my way; but soon I gave preference to the distractions of the good old angling game. Strikes came readily. I fought until I was tired.

Fortunately I had my heavy tackle with thirty-nine-thread line. I lost several fish by having the hook pull out, but I did not break a line. I accounted for five tuna, none over 135 pounds, though I had no lack of exercise and hard work with any of them.

For a while during that day there was a strange launch at hand. I was too busy to take notice of what its anglers were doing, but I did observe that one of them was repeatedly breaking off fish and that while in my vicinity neither made catches.

That evening, two gentlemen from the Los Angeles yacht called on us and showed considerable interest in the tuna we had taken. They told us they had been fishing for several days, had caught some small tuna, but had not been successful in stopping the large ones. Upon learning they were using the twenty-four-thread line, we explained how impractical we found it and how superior the thirty-nine-thread proved.

I brought my tackle for examination. One of the men showed no particular interest, but the other studied it very carefully. I think the latter respected it, for our catch of tuna had opened his eyes.

The market fishermen were glad to take all the tuna we could bring in, which in turn pleased us. To them our contributions meant money without effort; to us, no waste of fish, no conscience pangs for catching large numbers of them.

After the experience of this day, Z. G. insisted upon the heaviest tackle and thirty-nine-thread line for all. It was necessary to make our own baits. The hooks of the baits we had purchased would not hold. A big tuna would twist them from the wood with one savage shake of his head. We tried out several baits. They were all fairly good, but the most successful one was a large hook concealed by white feathers and attached to a heavy wire leader.

Our second day was no less interesting than the first. A westerly wind and choppy sea made uncomfortable fishing conditions, yet did not in any way lessen the appetites of the tuna. Smashing strikes were inevitably in order. Those of us who still hung hopes on other commercial baits, dug up from our supplies, saw them sadly disfigured and their worthlessness brutally demonstrated.

Disasters mounted as the day advanced. Romer lost several of his specially made baits before he finally hooked a tuna solidly. This one turned out to be the star performer of the day, and gave Romer the hardest fight of his life. His comment, when we suggested that this fish was small compared with those yet due him, was, "I don't care to tackle another of that size very soon, thank you."

We were elated to find his tuna weighed 184 pounds. Captain Mitchell and Z. G. brought in eight tuna that evening, the largest 171 pounds, and there were two very nice fish to my credit.

A few chats with the market fishermen gave us all kinds of information about their end of the tuna industry. They were engaged in three styles of fishing. Three boats were busy at purse-seines, three were kept strictly to trolling, and six were given exclusively to the live-bait fishing. The purse-seine boats were earning, at this time, from twelve to sixteen hundred dollars per day. The trolling boats were making little short of that, and the men on the bait boats had averaged four hundred dollars per man per week for the past five months. It is an obvious conclusion that market fishing at Cape San Lucas is very profitable.

The captain of the cannery schooner had been receiving fish there for the past eight years. He told us he saw no diminution in the number of yellow-fin tuna; that year after year they ran in great numbers, and thousands of tons were caught annually. It seems the market men prefer the smaller ones, but take all sizes, many weighing up to 300 pounds. Despite his assurance, I wondered if in a number of years to come an appreciable depletion of supply would not be evident.

We wanted Romer to continue his tuna fishing with us, but on the morning after his 184-pound catch he was in no mood for big-game sea fishing. He declared he needed a rest and thought he would try some shore fishing, so he rigged up his little launch with suitable light tackle and started for a trip around the bay. He returned at night with a wild tale of adventure. He had several fights with large white sea bass, and lost an easily sixty-pound yellowtail after a trying hour.

The small fish he hooked became unanticipated baits for larger ones. One incident of this kind turned into a long two-hour fight. Romer, describing it, said:

"I never thought I could catch that fish. I never knew rock bass grew so large, and fighting it on three-six tackle, I was sure at a disadvantage. My hands and fingers gave out, and I was almost dead, but I finally got him, a sixty-six pounder! What do you know about that? Then we nearly swamped the boat in a fight with a giant ray, but it got away. There were any number of big red snappers. Never for a single moment during the whole day was there a lull in fishing. It sure was great!"

Cape San Lucas was another pinnacle in fishing experience. Each place we visited seemed the true Mecca; we became confounded when trying to name the best of our late fishing-grounds. At the cape the sea teemed with life. Schools of porpoise visited daily, black fish rolled on the surface, sharks—particularly hammerheads and leopards—were ever present, and enormous black-and-white rays startled us now and again by jumping clear and making complete turns in the air; almost any time a whale could be seen blowing, while far out to sea and everywhere round us were splashes of feeding tuna.

Z. G. and Captain Mitchell were running a race for tuna honors, both size and number. I could not keep abreast of their boats while I was fishing, and therefore they had to review their adventures when we gathered on the *Fisherman*. They had successive red-letter days —one when they courted Lady Luck by taking several hundred-pound tuna early in the day, and then to avoid these baby weights going farther to sea, where they found a school of big fellows that kept them as busy as they cared to be.

The first of these Z. G. hooked. It took him three-quarters of an hour to bring the fish to gaff. It was a 174-pound beauty. Next Captain Mitchell came in for a grueling fight of over two hours, which had its moments of threatening disaster but ended in victory over a slim tuna of 184-pound weight.

Z. G.'s second strike afforded the most wonderful run of the day. The tuna shot over the surface, showing above water most of the time till he had twelve hundred feet of line out, and fast as they did chase him, they could not gain anything. For some mighty thrilling moments a hundred yards of line were above water, which is unusual, since tuna generally sound quickly when they are hooked.

He settled down at last to a three-and-a-half-hour fight, at many moments precarious to the extreme for Z. G., which proved his species as game as any blue-fin tuna in the Seven Seas. It took Captain Mitchell and the boatmen together to lift him aboard. He was over seven feet in length and weighed 318 pounds. This is the record for yellow-fin tuna.

The same day was about the hardest I ever put in. Seven tuna fell to my rod, three of them just a few pounds short of 200.

Late in the afternoon, when I was very spent and weary, I hooked an eighth tuna. He sounded to a great depth, and stayed there. I could not budge him. I was about to give up when I felt something take him, and a strange vibration came up the line, acting almost like an electric shock on me; then at my line dragged an inconceivably dead weight. I thought of an immense shark, but there was no accompanying movement, as is usual when a shark takes a fish.

It was the strangest sensation—a dragging powerful weight, as if I were hooked to the bottom of an unfathomed sea. Presently I felt a kind of mauling or rolling movement of my fish. The boatman took the line in his hand, but could not lift an inch. "Something powerful heavy!" he declared. "Must be a thousand pounds!"

We agreed on the advantage of our strange opponent for a while, and then commenced a struggle to make him yield a little. It was strenuous labor. In time we lifted the line a few inches, and with the slowest of progress continued to work it up. In half an hour we felt hopeful of results and anticipated hauling the imposter to view. Patiently we toiled, and although greatly excited we were exceedingly careful.

Then suddenly the great weight was released. Only the tuna was on, and he inactive. We pulled him up, a 175-pound fish, stone dead! Not a movement of any kind! He was scarred. Around his body was a continuous circular welt which looked like the binding mark of a rope, and the skin was broken in places. He had been in the clutches of an octopus. There was no doubt of it. I remember the story of the Florida boatman who had a terrible fight with an octopus which had attached itself to his boat. He managed to get free, after an uncanny experience, only by cutting off the tentacles with an ax.

What a trying but incomparable day for me!

That night there was great excitement in the bay among the market fishing-boats, and also on the *Fisherman*, over the catch of a wonderful Marlin swordfish by one of the market men. He was trolling for tuna with a white rag as bait when the Marlin took hold.

We called to see the fish, a gigantic specimen over twelve feet in length and of an estimated weight of 600 pounds. The market fishermen reported seeing seven others during the day, and thereby ruined our peace of mind. We immediately developed swordfish fever, and the next few days I spent trolling the ocean with teasers

The Author with Two Big Yellowfins Close to 200 Pounds

AVERAGE WEIGHT, 185 POUNDS

out for Marlin. I was not very successful, but managed to raise a few, one of them a whale of a black fellow that followed the teasers for a long time but refused the various baits I offered.

I finally had the fortune to take a Marlin of 170 pounds, the only one caught during our trip. They were all curious about the teasers and baits, but for some reason did not care to bite. Perhaps at the time in that latitude it was off season for Marlin strikes. They are very finicky. Often when they first appear at Catalina, in late summer, they ignore our lures consistently.

Discouraged by the Marlins' antics, we returned to tuna fishing. I reached the point where, from sheer exhaustion, I would have to refuse to put a bait in the water. A bait of any kind—feathers, plug, rag baby, or cut bait—was hungrily devoured.

I watched a double-header fight in which Z. G. and Captain Mitchell were engaged over an hour. It was a case of changing seats and carefully untangling lines and rods while the fight waged its hottest. Wonderful to relate, they landed both tuna. On the next double-header, which occurred very soon, Captain Mitchell broke his rod off at the butt. Nothing daunted, this gentleman went after the tuna by the hand-line method, and while Z. G. worked laboriously at his rod Captain Mitchell climbed back and forth over the boat, hauling on the tuna, going it hand over hand, at what seemed an endless task, but came to a happy termination.

Again they saved both tuna. This proved that I was not the only angler in the party who fell heir to the epithet "lucky."

On the heels of this incident Z. G. hooked a powerful tuna and fought him for two hours. It is impossible to relate all that happened in the boat that day. Space would not permit it. But evening saw two tired, spent anglers returning with eleven tuna, seven for Z. G. and four for Captain Mitchell. Z. G.'s largest weighed 215 pounds. The others ran between 198 and 170 pounds. Captain Mitchell's ran 202, 175, 165, 145. They had made the greatest catch of tuna ever recorded.

Our visiting anglers from Los Angles called on us this evening to say good-by, for they were homeward bound. They congratulated us on our methods, and admitted that of the one hundred feather jigs with which they had started only six remained. Experience is a relentless teacher. Months later I learned that these men had loaded up with heavy rods and thirty-nine-thread line and returned to Cape San Lucas, where their second visit gave very satisfactory results.

I was beginning to feel reluctant about fighting so many large tuna. My hands were in bad condition, and my back rebelled at the unremitting strain, so I was glad when the tuna let up striking for a few days and I got some much-needed rest. I followed Z. G.'s boat closely during this time. Between us we raised seven Marlin, one of which fooled Z. G. after a short fight. There were no sailfish about nor any broadbill swordfish, but we did have an enviable chase after acres of blackfish and procured some remarkable photographs.

At the very end of our stay at Cape San Lucas it fell to me to furnish sufficient excitement to please everybody. I was lazily working four or five miles offshore when I saw a great fin or tail rise out of the sea. I thought of whales, orca, blackfish, but this thing in the distance was new and strange. We ran near and found it to be some tremendous fish or mammal, with tail standing three feet above water.

The other boat was so far off that we decided to explore alone, much to my regret afterward. We drew very close. Presently we descried a body much longer than my thirty-two-foot launch. The creature, which was so entirely new to me that for lack of other name I called shark, was very round of body and had white spots on its back. The boatmen wanted to harpoon it, but I figured it would be a hopeless task, so would not consent.

Just for the fun of it I suggested that we might tie a long rope to our big gaff and gaff it through the tail. The boys were only too anxious. We rigged up the gaff and, running up behind our shark, I stuck it through the top of his tail. He displayed his objection by flipping said appendage, the spread of which was fifteen feet, and throwing enough water to nearly sink the boat.

I felt rather weak and small, but I held on to the rope as the monster sounded. He went down about three hundred feet, then accommodatingly returned to the surface and started off to sea with us. He took us at a slow tow with little effort or commotion. This new brand of sport continued for half an hour and I began to think the joke was on me. In the meantime Z. G. had noticed that something was amiss and was coming toward us.

As he came up I yelled: "Some fish! Bigger than my boat and doesn't mind us at all!"

He grinned and rejoined: "You're a bright one! There's no chance in the world of getting that thing. It's a *Rhineodon typus*. Why, he's sixty feet long, and he'll weigh tons!"

"He's the toughest-looking proposition I ever saw on the ocean," I returned. "And that's a pretty mean name they've given him."

Fighting blood had been aroused aboard my launch. We made a murderous-looking weapon, of an iron, to which we tied six hundred feet of rope, and straightway approached for another attack. When we plunged the iron into the creature, there was a roar in the water, a

ADVENTURES OF A DEEP-SEA ANGLER

mighty splash as the tail just missed our boat, and then a big whirling hole where he sounded. The rope paid out slowly, and the fish stopped before the full length was taken. We moved up toward him and regained the line, and getting an equal strain on both ropes we hung on.

Then we suggested collecting harpoons, ropes, and guns from the ship and trying our luck in earnest. By promising we would stay a safe distance from the *Rhineodon* until he returned, we coaxed Z. G. to get the full array of paraphernalia. We fought the *Rhineodon typus* for an hour and a half while the other launch was gone, but did not make the slightest impression on him. He towed us about four miles, and we were getting well out to sea.

I anxiously watched for Z. G.'s return and was relieved when I saw his boat plowing the ocean at full speed, spray flying everywhere. I could see, too, that the boat was loaded with men—Captain Mitchell, Romer, and several others. We certainly needed them.

We divided the men and equipment, taking some on our boat, and soon had another iron rigged up and ready for business. As the iron entered the fish he protested as vigorously as before, with the same threshing tail action which left us drenched. Presently he was riding both launches over the ocean. They might well have been light surfboards attached to a large tug.

Much confusion prevailed amid the shouting of orders. The *Rhineodon* swam under the boat and gave us a terrible scare. I felt then the utter futility of coping with the monster. Again he sounded, this time to great depth. Everybody strained with all his might, but the lines slipped away swiftly and surely. At sixteen hundred feet he stopped his descent and started us off on another long voyage.

The hours passed. What was begun in sport became a

Z. G.'s Biggest Allison Tuna, 318 Pounds. Note the Long Fins

HAVING FUN FUSSING OVER TACKLE

definite ordeal. Recovering the rope was slow and strenuous work. The men were dripping with perspiration and sea spray, and they slid about on slippery decks. It took an hour of relentless work to pull the creature to the surface. I was completely done; so I took the wheel.

Five times that *Rhineodon* sounded. Then came sunset, and as if that was his hour to quit surface play, he turned tail and started for the bottom in a startlingly thorough business-like manner. It was a caution the way those ropes paid out! Five hundred feet! . . . One thousand feet! Two tubs tied at that length went over and out of sight. At fifteen hundred feet we knew something would soon break. Still he took rope!

The men strove with all their strength to stave off disaster. It was inevitable! We tied on the last piece of rope and made a final herculean effort to stop the fish. But we failed. I yelled to half-hitch the rope on the tow post and await results. The boat pitched, and it looked as though she might go down. Then the irons came out. What a great relief! The battle was over.

I sank in a corner. I seemed to be insensible to my fatigue for a time. I was possessed with the thought of the *Rhineodon typus* and kept saying to myself again and again: "What a wonderful fish! And what a mighty fighter!"

## CHAPTER XII

## BIG FISH OF NEW ZEALAND

MY BROTHER made two trips to New Zealand, fishing adventures both, the first the rainbow quest, the second a span of the rainbow to explore what treasure it held. Having found fish in abundance over a limited area on his first visit, he at once planned a return on which he would investigate whether or not what was true of one small region of the coast was true of the whole, and invited me to help him in the back-breaking job. Hence another cruise on the *Fisherman*, and the opportunity to troll waters that had never been touched by any other angler.

We caught swordfish off the Kara-Kara Islands almost to the North Cape, the first fish ever taken so far north; then going south we anchored and fished at every available place on the coast. For days we tried out the Reefs, grounds four miles off Whangaroa and known to few men, and after that we scoured around the Cavalli Islands, in the Bay of Islands off Cape Brett, and on down to Moko Hinau and Great Barrier Islands, and south to Tauranga in the Bay of Plenty. The three hundred miles we covered offered the best fishing for large fish of any place we have yet discovered.

Z. G. had found that New Zealanders fished exclusively by drifting. Drifting is a time-honored method, but it has its specific uses, with no more universal application than have the habits of fish for which men angle. For instance, it might be the means of hooking some leviathan that lives deep down and invariably fights deep down. It certainly is the best way of hooking very

[ 148 ]

heavy sharks, such as the reremai and the thresher. But what of the joy of tempting a surface-feeder like the swordfish with a bait that skims the surface, of actually seeing him on its trail and sometimes fighting off another comer? What of the skill in coaxing him to follow it, of inspiring him against fish sense to chase it out of bounds of a surer meal? What of the transcendent thrill, the climax of foregone suspense, when he finally takes it and the fight is on? Who would prefer to feel a deep-down tug on a drifting bait and find his homely satis-faction in the thought that whatever has taken the bait—and who ever knows what has?—happened on it quite by accident? No one who has known the former method.

The teaser (persuader, one native erroneously called it, grasping its purpose if not its correct nomenclature) was unheard of in New Zealand until Z. G.'s first visit there. It caused many a sly wink, I understand; but the turn came for our laughing winks when, the next year, we counted seven boats in one day off Cape Brett, all trolling with teasers out in the fashion we had prescribed. Greater power to those men who tried it and granted its superiority in the face of local conservatism! Fishing is no individual nation's sport; it is universal. Anyone who can add to the pleasure and proficiency of this healthful, youth-lending avocation, be he Eskimo or Zulu, will find me ready to learn his ways and means.

The possibilities of New Zealand waters for angling are boundless. The surface has been only scratched, and the next few years will probably show splendid advance-ment in angling methods, and certainly remarkable re-sults. Swordfish and mako well over a thousand pounds will yet be taken. Witness Captain Mitchell's world-record black Marlin, world-record weight of all other fish weights, caught on the trip with my brother the first year.

No doubt fish of this size have often been hooked. Reports are numerous of extremely heavy ones that have never shown on the surface and have smashed to pieces all present-day tackle. Maybe some were giant tuna, for certain antics described to me are peculiar to that heroic fighter. No tackle made in New Zealand at the present time is going to stop a 1,000-pound tuna in her deep coastal waters.

The primal need of an angler anywhere is bait—the choicest bait for the fish he is after—and he must know where to get it. In most places in New Zealand Nature provides for this need most generously. She beckons you to acres of small fish, schools of kahawai and trevalli, ever denoted by clouds of birds hovering over them. There beneath these schools you see for yourself the story of double pursuit when larger species smash through feeding. When fishing for bait with light tackle you are always in danger of having some snatched from your hook by the big fellows. I suggest a tourist's ad, such as, "To bait your hook and lure your fish in a single action, come to New Zealand!"

But it is no fun if you hook a deep-sea fish on a very light bait tackle. A swordfish or a mako or a yellowtail or a shark can smash everything for you in quick order.

On several occasions I drifted New Zealand fashion at places where schools of bait would come by, possibly attended by a large fish. Never knowing what prowled below, if anything, the actual strike was always unanticipated. When it came you were either surprised in short order by a swordfish or mako jump, or left to debate whether the fish which persisted in deep-down fighting was a yellowtail or one of a number of varieties of common sharks. If you were hooked to a large reremai or a thresher shark the fight might last hours. A New Zea-

The "Fisherman" at Anchor in Bay of Islands, New Zealand

A School of Kakawai (Bait)

lander had a fight with a reremai which lasted from noon till midnight.

Z. G. and Captain Mitchell had each had their fights with big reremai, fish of over 700 pounds, and they were keen to see the new member of the party try it. It was my good fortune to meet with only a small one, 350 pounds, but I had all I wanted. He went down to watch the mermaids comb their hair and refused to leave, and I had to lift him from the floor of the sea. When I got through with him I was dripping wet all over and my spine was out of whack. I thank my lucky star I never hooked a big one.

My brother was anxious to have his boy meet with one of these sulkers. Romer, assured of his strength, was keen to tackle big fish. "Bring them on!" he would challenge us. "I'll show you!"

One day when Romer was fishing with him, Z. G. hooked a very heavy, powerful fish and without admitting he thought it was a reremai, he turned the rod over to Romer. I was near at the time and stayed around to see the fun. Up to that time Romer had never caught a swordfish. His largest fish, bar sharks, had been his 184-pound Cape San Lucas tuna, so a fish of probably 500 pounds or more was a new experience. I was sure Z. G. was putting over a trick on him.

Romer's battle proved one of the hardest I ever witnessed, but a royal one. After he put in two exhausting hours we discovered he was hung to a tremendous thresher shark. What a situation! Z. G. had always wanted to catch a large thresher, and here was his chance gone—passed idly over—because, for once, his sagacity failed him.

Though Romer knew a formidable fight lay ahead, he refused to give up the rod. There were no long runs, there was no jumping—nothing spectacular; only a fight deep down with a monster who refused to die.

I felt sorry for Romer. He was suffering. His face, his every action showed the strain under which he toiled, but he was game and fought on. Finally he lifted the thresher to the place where the wire leader could be reached. Strong hands grabbed it and held on. The end was near. Another minute, and the shark was gaffed and tied. Try as they did, six husky men could not hoist it on the boat.

Romer, more dead than alive, still had strength to appreciate the situation and to laugh at his perplexed father in devilish joy and half-apology. The magnificent thresher shark that caused all the strife and consternation weighed 640 pounds.

Very large yellowtail follow the schools of bait. At Catalina, years ago, when yellowtail fishing was at its best, fish of thirty-five and forty pounds were considered large. The largest ever caught there was something like sixty pounds. In New Zealand sixty, eighty, ninety, and one hundred pounders are fairly casual catches. Some over a hundred pounds have been taken and there is no doubt that they run even larger. My brother has the record, 111 pounds. As fighters they equal the best game fish. Taking three or four of these yellowtail as a side play for heavier events makes a strenuous day.

Sometimes we drew large seines in the coves and shallow waters, and besides bait netted many excellent food fish, such as snappers and flounders. Mullet, a most attractive lure for New Zealand fish, we caught at night by setting a gill net.

It was always interesting to follow Captain Mitchell's little boat. When business was dull with the rest of us, invariably action centered round the Captain. He is what you might call a hearty fisherman. He takes on any kind

The Author Fast to His First New Zealand Swordfish

ZANE GREY HOOKED TO BLACK MARLIN

of a fish or shark with gusto. Swordfish and mako seem eager for a fighting acquaintance with him. Trolling, drifting, or sleeping, good fortune camps on his trail.

Captain's great ambition was to take a hammerhead shark, a nice big fellow. He never passed one without trying a bait on him. Usually he hooked them; some he lost through breaking of leaders and lines, but finally he took one over 400 pounds weight.

Occasionally strangers supplied entertainment for us without altruistic intent, and such was the case with a very serious English angler whom we watched battling with a mako. The fish jumped repeatedly, making, as only a mako can, wonderful somersaults in the air. After a while he jumped free, trailing line behind him. The outraged angler flung his rod down and hurried from the scene.

Half an hour later Captain Mitchell was hooked to that very same mako. Every time the fish jumped we could see our late neighbor's leader flying in the air. It was a short, hard fight. The Captain soon tied up a fine mako, well over 300 pounds. Then he rescued the original leader and went in search of the unfortunate angler who had lost it. In a most matter-of-fact way he asked the man if he had lost one recently.

"Yes, and it was a damn large mako that took it," the man returned.

Captain, grinning like a youngster, proffered the leader, explained that he had come especially to return it, and showed the man the mako he had missed.

It was Captain Mitchell's big Marlin that nearly jumped into the camera man's boat, giving an unparalleled opportunity for thrilling motion pictures. This aggressive Marlin gloried in his ability and the sheer strength of his powerful body. He had a thousand feet of line out when he decided to show all onlookers what

he could do. He circled the boat with breath-taking speed
and in long greyhound leaps went straight for the camera
man, who was grinding happily.

The boatmen waited daringly late, but in the nick of
time hooked up the power and got away. Another minute and the fish would have come aboard. The last jump
actually filled the finder of the camera. On the screen
the Marlin shows in ultra-large close-up.

Z. G. was keen for a large mako, and particularly for
photographs of a mako in the air. I followed him for
many days, watched many encounters, and saw some
wonderful jumping. He caught a number, and finally one
of 418 pounds. Old speed-king mako defied us to do
much with our cameras, particularly the motion pictures,
though one of our ordinary photographs shows his acrobatics to remarkable advantage. But there will come another year when he will tell his story in motion.

Off the Cavalli Islands, Z. G. had a splendid day of
Marlin fishing. A very large school of bait was being
harassed by big fish, and as often as Z. G. could get a
bait down under the school a big Marlin would take it.
Off to sea the fish would go, leaping all the way, with
Z. G. following rapidly. In a half hour, back would come
the boat, flag flying and Marlin on board. Three times
this performance was repeated, and three large Marlin
lay aboard the busy boat before the bait, in frantic search
for shelter, had disappeared from our horizon.

Romer hooked his first Marlin while fishing from my
boat. He was cool and unconcerned and played his fish
well. Perhaps I made it a little easier for him than I
should have by taking charge of the boat and its handling.
It was a good fight, and I was glad to hear him shout
each time the Marlin made a beautiful leap or started
away on a long run.

Another day Romer took two, but these not so easily.

R. C.'s Largest Marlin, 368 Pounds

R. C. and Captain Mitchell

They were hard fighters, given little to jumping and much to deep-down stubborn play. Romer showed very marked signs of distress on the second one, and he had a great deal more respect for those he caught later.

On his first trip, Z. G. caught the first broadbill ever taken in New Zealand waters. The second year Mr. Fred Burnham of San Francisco took one which weighed 453 pounds. Now, with reports current that a number were seen this year, it is sensible to assume that broadbill fishing will soon be an added attraction for both local and foreign anglers.

I saw one large broadbill myself. I was with Zane at the time. I spotted the fish first, though it is seldom I can snatch this honor from my brother. It looked like a very large broadbill, and Z. G. was keen to hook him. He worked him carefully with a fine large bait, but he could not induce him to take it. Time and again he tried, only to have the fish veer away. We gave up coaxing and ran up on him to have a look. He was a husky giant, fully 800 or 900 pounds. In the clear water, with the sun shining on him, he was magnificent to see. He swam lazily on the surface as we approached, showing little fear of the boat until we were almost on him, when he gave his tail a flip and disappeared.

Not all the Pacific Ocean deserves the name Balboa bestowed on it when, from his northerly stand, he gazed on the vast placid sea. He would have chosen another name if he had come upon it by a southerly route. I'll never forget the day we made the trip from Whangaroa to Great Barrier Island with the *Fisherman* and the native launches, and Captain Mitchell in the *Sky Blue*, his small craft from the ship.

The native launches, built for stormy home waters, were larger and sturdier than ours. Z. G. wanted to hoist the *Sky Blue* aboard before we set out, but Captain

Mitchell preferred to make the journey in the launch. The weather seemed fair and the barometer not at all alarming, but when we were well on our way we ran into a heavy gale. The *Fisherman* rolled and tossed hour after hour. There were clatter and bang from the galley, where presently the cook despaired of serving any meals. Everything movable on the ship had to be lashed down.

All the while the launches rode within our horizon, though sometimes distantly, and the *Sky Blue* plunged and soared and swayed and rolled, every other minute disappearing in the trough of a wave. I managed to keep on deck; I was too concerned to go below.

Grimly, minute after minute, I watched for that small boat's rise, dreading that one time it might not come up. There was nothing to do. In such a sea the men could not board the *Fisherman*. To be sure, the other launches were on hand, but what were the chances of a rescue if the *Sky Blue* capsized?

That terrible day belongs to the past. Kindly Providence saved the Captain and his boatmen and brought their worthy battling boat to safe harbor. No more such folly, we agreed. Always rough days outnumbered the pleasant calm ones in these waters, and we should have distrusted the weather.

A rough sea is my undoing. Many a time I returned to the *Fisherman* from our daily excursions utterly, miserably seasick and worn from trying to hang aboard. But I was so anxious to get results I went out regardless of conditions. So much can happen in New Zealand waters you hate to risk losing some choice opportunity. Who can tell what day the big mako or striped Marlin or giant black Marlin will come in?

New Zealand Marlin average much larger than those in California or Mexico waters. Seldom you see one less than 200 pounds. The average run is about 260 pounds,

THIS ONE NEARLY CAME ABOARD

MARLIN THROWING BAIT

while the largest caught to date weighed 450. The striped Marlin, however, must not be confounded with the black Marlin, his giant cousin, first found and named by my brother.

I was always alert when Marlin approached my bait, and I had the good fortune to hook every one that struck. With fifteen hundred feet of thirty-nine line and a heavier rod than the one I use in California, I felt confident. I believe the Marlin of New Zealand are really faster than the ones at Catalina. Almost every one would take from eight hundred to one thousand feet of line on the first run, making it necessary for me to follow them. Size might contribute to speed with this species.

My first Marlin, one of 271 pounds, jumped fifty-six times. It was a great exhibition. We had to turn the boat and run full speed to keep up with him. I caught one by drifting in the prescribed New Zealand fashion, but I missed the thrill that our own method gives. Many a time while trolling, three or four Marlin would rise to the teasers, and all hands would have a merry time for a few minutes trying to rescue the teasers and attract the fish to the bait.

Now when I dwell on the pleasure of New Zealand fishing, the uncomfortable times slough from memory, and I think of a day of bright sunshine when the sea was gentle, the ocean alive with fish, and armies of white birds were charging many detachments of migrating bait. That day's first Marlin rushed to his doom, in fact almost climbed aboard the boat.

I was letting my bait down into the water when he shot out directly astern, grabbed it furiously, and tore off on a run. I looked up in time to see two other great Marlin, heavy as the first, rushing the teasers and pulling at them. Even before I could act, my fish was in the air.

Then he gave me a ride that was hard to beat, directly out to sea on a two-mile race. Happily, I was the one who finished.

This fish had struck suddenly because he was accompanied by other Marlin. I have often noticed that a Marlin shows no hesitancy about rushing a bait if there is any chance of competition. Alone he almost always hits the bait three or four times, and then takes it slowly.

My second Marlin hit the bait like a thunderbolt and hooked himself. He, too, went directly out to sea. I was gone another hour, and again returned a victor. He was of good weight—240 pounds, we later learned. I began to feel hilarious, and I put up a couple of flags to celebrate the occasion. I had passed Captain Mitchell far out, hooked on and fighting, and Z. G. was loading a black Marlin.

The swordfish were jumping so actively that I decided to try to photograph the next one with my motion-picture camera. I tied my rod on the chair and laid my camera beside me. I intended, on hooking another fish, to drop the rod, grab the camera, and trust to luck to give me action and spare all possible disaster.

I had more of a job than I had planned for. Not just one Marlin but many came, seven or eight in a lively school, bent for my bait and teasers. Beautiful gleams of purple, like stray lightning flashes, they crossed and recrossed behind me. What an onslaught! I saw my teasers disappear in the mouths of hungry fish, and the next moment I left my seat unanticipatedly.

I struck, dropped the rod, and felt for my camera. I watched the sea where my Marlin flared through. He was upright on his tail, actually walking the water at terrific speed and describing a circle round the boat. The bait swung free, a foot up on the leader.

ROMER WITH HIS GREAT THRESHER SHARK, 640 POUNDS

Z. G. AND WORLD-RECORD STRIPED MARLIN, 450 POUNDS

My rod bobbed about, uncontrolled. The reel screeched. I gripped the motion-picture machine in hands hard to steady. Then the clatter of my rod and reel awoke me to the fact that the Marlin was dashing far afield. Scant feet of line were whizzing off my reel toward their end. I snatched the rod. We turned the boat and threw her into full power. The engines roared. I wonder my line did not break from the strain. I wound madly; my wrists grew numb. In the excitement of photographing, I had no thought of the Marlin's size, but the boatman said he was a fine one.

Presently I gained on the fish sufficient distance to make fair fight possible. What an exhilarating experience! What a gratifying outlook! As fair a sea as a man could ask for, sunny skies and rugged coastline, and birds soaring and drifting between me and a great antagonist whom my muscles cried for. I was vaguely aware of spectators, native anglers and Englishmen and Australians, watching me battle. What happened to time? I don't know. Perhaps it stood still and started again when I helped to pull the fish aboard.

I have always been considered a lucky Marlin fisherman. My catch of seven in one day, years ago at Catalina, still keeps the lead, although Z. G. has taken five and Captain Mitchell six. No doubt they will some day beat me in New Zealand waters, where the chances for such a catch are most possible.

The great Marlin that I almost sacrificed for pictures weighed 368 pounds. He was the largest I have ever caught, eclipsing my Catalina Marlin of 354 pounds. Incidentally, he was the largest striped Marlin taken by our party from the southern waters.

Summing up the total catch of the three boats while in New Zealand, omitting the undesirable reremai, we found we had taken sixty-three swordfish and mako, and one giant thresher. This is a fair record in the light of forty-two days of bad weather, a poor season on a normally temperamental sea, when time and again conditions prohibited fishing.

CHAPTER XIII

THE MAKO

I NEVER did like sharks. I never thought the time
would come when I would hail one of this species as
a great fish, put in hours fighting him with great gusto
and thrill, and then, in mere man's inadequate way, try
to tell something about his baffling kind. But my hat is
off. If I had voice in the matter, I would not call him a
shark. Sharks, on the whole, despite their destructive pursuits, are pitifully poor sports, sulk and do not fight when
hooked, and yield to defeat earlier than other deep-sea
fish. Not so with the mako.

The mako is never found in northern waters; he fre-
quents the antipodes only. He is torpedo-shaped and
built for speed, has a bullet-shaped head, large protrud-
ing eyes, and huge jaws with several rows of long triangular teeth, like prongs on a mowing-machine, that
cut and shred and grind mercilessly. Boatmen claim that
the teeth of the back rows continually supply forward
rows whenever a tooth is missing. After examination of
a mako's jaw, such process seems probable, though in
your amazement at his vicious-looking armament you feel
old mako could afford to lose many teeth before his diges-
tion would be impaired.

He is built to survive in his natural habitat, and to
face man with his ferocity and power. As a jumper he
outclasses every fish in the sea.

My first information concerning the mako came from
my brother on his return from his first trip to New Zealand. Mighty indeed were his reports. He laughed at my

[ 161 ]

skepticism. Then the time arrived when I came and saw and—well, the rest goes with the story.

Z. G. was sure he had found the El Dorado for all anglers, and he boasted of the magical waters of this foreign country with all the flare of a Los Angeles real-estate agent who is going to sell you something or die. I pretended indifference, though I knew when my brother gets worked up to that pitch there is a reason. But when Z. G. returned to New Zealand and toted me along for what he promised would be the trip of my life, as I have already admitted I learned he was right.

The Bay of Islands, our first anchorage after the *Fisherman* had cleared port at Auckland, was so beautiful that I would have been content to accept any claim whatever for New Zealand's natural scenery. Here the sea had encroached upon a thousand hills, separating them into islands, cutting in bays and coves, and building crescent beaches. The *Fisherman* rode in the snug harbor of a thousand-acre island, looking out in one direction to a greater bay that led to the sea, and elsewhere to the hummocky hills that made our shelter so secure. The slopes were covered with a gold-colored grass about the height of oats, which rippled all day in the breeze, ever on and up over the hilltops, in progressive motion similar to that of the sea.

There were sweeps of trees and shrubs. The *ti* tree, commonly called New Zealand heather, had a delicate pink-and-white bloom. The *tii-tii* tree, a slender semi-tropical growth much like a fringed palm, had a long bare trunk capped with full-bunched foliage, clusters of long fronds that rustled in the slightest breeze. The tropical fern tree, a long slender trunk with a burst of tremendous ferns at its tip-top point, made a lacy green canopy against the sun.

Most beautiful of all was the *pohutukawa*. It was a

The "Fisherman" Going into Whangaroa, New Zealand

The Leaping Mako

wide-spreading tree, gnarled and aged. Its dark, glistening leaves reminded me of the Florida mangroves. The name of this tree, lovely in sound when given the Maori accent, means "washed by the sea spray," a felicitous name, since it grows so close to the shore that during storms it actually catches the spray from the breaking waves. Christmas tree is the English nomenclature for the *pohutukawa*, so called because it has a gorgeous shower of red bloom just before Christmas. The most sheltered trees hold their flaming glory till late January.

Idling in our secluded haven, it was hard to believe that a ten-minute run would bring us to the booming surf outside. And what a vastly different prospect there! A bold, rugged coastline, solitary buttes and isolated islands with precipitous rock walls, and the insurgent sea beating itself to white foam against all barriers. Calm days were rare that season, a sad fact for me, as my deep-sea fishing laurels come only through stubbornly fighting seasickness. However, my interest had been stimulated to the point where no odds were too great to conquer.

I started my New Zealand fishing with a right good will. The very first time we ran out to try our luck, I saw marvelous schools of bait, and that was all the promise I needed. These bait fish—*kahawai* and *trevalli*—rode the surface in swift-moving patches, each an acre in itself. Whenever a big fish charged from underneath, they turned with remarkable unified precipitation, casting clouds of spray everywhere, and the clatter they made was like that of shattering glass magnified to a deafening roar.

Working continuously over these schools were thousands of beautiful white gulls. Life for the bait fish is a perpetual race to escape from enemies that crowd from both above and below. Those which survive reproduce their kind, giving them this hectic heritage of eternal struggle.

My first days in New Zealand waters were not fruitful so far as my own fishing was concerned, but I was much interested in the things that were going on around me, and particularly in what the other boats were doing. The records established the previous year by my brother and Captain Mitchell had made me feel that almost anything could happen, so I was not averse to starting slowly.

One day while watching Captain Mitchell, who was fishing safely remote from my trolling-ground, I saw a very large fish jump twice, close behind his boat. It was the nature of his leaps that amazed me. Such propulsion! Such speed and grace! Such daring challenge! That performance was strange to me. I ran Captain Mitchell's way, but everything was serene by the time I got there. Captain was fishing again and puffing away on his pipe.

"Hey!" I yelled. "What's going on over here?"

Captain laughed. "Did you see that bird jump? Mako! About four hundred pounds, the beggar! Bit my leader in two. Some fish, this mako."

There was no disputing Captain's closing remark. "That sight was enough to give me the mako itch," I rejoined.

And it was. From that moment I concentrated on mako with a fervor which should have driven any other kind of fish from my bait. There were times of misgiving when I wondered what I would do with a 1,000-pound fish of such might and ferocity. And a 1,000 pounder was not the largest we might hook.

I had a young boy to run my boat who, though a good engineer, was not an experienced boatman. In fact, this was his first season. To offset this disadvantage, I inveigled the first mate of the *Fisherman* to accompany me on my daily expeditions. He had been a market fisher-

This Mako Had Wings

Towing Mako In

THE MAKO

man in California and was sufficiently versed in fish antics to prove valuable in emergency.

I had been told that the mako was a bad actor around the boat, and had to be gaffed and tied quickly before he got second wind. The first mako fight I witnessed made my informant's warning seem mild.

After vigilant quest through many days, I found a mako surfacing. The New Zealand boatman told me to throw out a bait to him; said the fish had no fear of the boat and would take anything. This sounded well, but it did not work. Throwing the bait to him scared the mako and sent him down. I was terribly disappointed. I recovered only when I spotted him working up again.

Then I tried feeding him a bait in the manner we prescribe for swordfishing, trolling it some distance in front of him. This was effective. He saw the bait, swam under, and presently made a break to take it. I was aquiver with anticipation, and the instant I felt sure of him I lay on the hickory hard. I hooked him. He ran a short distance and sounded. I was puzzled. Where, pray, did the spectacular jumping come in?

I worked this fish back to the boat without much effort, such little effort, in fact, that I had misapprehensions about the mako's prowess. Taking no pains to conceal my disgust, I advised the boatman to get ready with the gaff. The boy took the leader and pulled the fish to the boat, and the mate reached for him with the gaff but missed. Whereupon the mako turned, made a strong rush, and sounded again. Even that seemed a tremendous bluff, for I soon pumped him back.

The mate gaffed him, and the gaff held. Then he reached for a rope, preparing to lasso the mako's tail. But the mako was no longer docile. With one terrific shake he tore free and shot off again, leaving us soaked and stuttering. This time he struck out with admirable de-

[ 165 ]

termination. I had my troubles stopping the run, and when I did he sounded. When I tried to lift him, he was a dead weight. I could not budge him. Something was wrong. He felt like a ton, yet I knew he could not weigh over 200 pounds.

After half an hour of hard work I brought him up broadside, tangled in the leader. This time we gaffed him successfully and tied him up. However, it was a long while before that stubborn fish died. It was embarrassing to have Z. G. watch that inglorious fight. He told me bluntly that we had made a terrible mess of the job. I agreed and promised a better exhibition at some future date.

I made good with my second mako, but what he did not do to me is not worth talking about. During the fight proper he was a game, savage opponent and put himself through a course of aquatic gymnastics that almost made me forget my part in the fray. Then at the climax he defied us to gaff him. When finally we did gaff and tie him, he threshed about, nearly wrecking the boat and me, too, and presently made a spectacular play for freedom that left us breathless.

At the time I was turned about in my chair with my rod under my arm, the butt still in the chair-socket. Suddenly I felt a tremendous shock and simultaneously was showered with water. I spun round like a top, chair and all, and then out of my chair against the side of the boat. I came within an inch of going overboard. The line was whizzing off the reel; the mako was making for the horizon, gaff torn out, but his tail still lassoed and trailing rope. It took time to play out his splendid courage, and when that was accomplished we dispatched him with a neater and quicker gaffing job.

I got that mako when he might easily have gotten me.

Had I pitched overboard, he might have taken me to sea with him, twined up in the line or leader, and sooner or later supplied a change in diet for his more healthy and less fatigued brothers.

The subject of sharks eating men has often been debated. I myself accept the facts and figures from people who have lived on the scenes of such tragedies. The pearl divers at the Perlas Islands in the Gulf of Panama lose about five men each year while hunting for pearls. In the Bay of Acapulco, old Mexico, vicious sharks have taken many lives.

Along New Zealand beaches, people swim with one eye seaward on the lookout for the deadly scavengers. No local tragedies occurred during my stay in New Zealand, but the papers reported three horrible catastrophes in Australia.

At Bronte, Miss Nita Derrett, a well-known swimmer, was seized by a shark. A young man promptly made efforts to rescue her and after a terrible encounter with the savage fish managed to save what was left of the girl. Both legs were severed from her body. Strange to relate, the girl recovered and to my knowledge is still living.

At Coogee, a bather was taken from a crowd of swimmers and never seen again. The attack was witnessed by several people from a high point above the bathing-beach.

At Manly Beach, the most popular swimming resort adjacent to Sidney, a shark took after a young man. His friend went to the rescue. In his attack, the friend landed on the shark's back, and he beat and cuffed the fish in an effort to tear his companion free. He succeeded in worsting the shark and brought in a sadly lacerated boy, one leg entirely gone. This poor victim died on the operating-table. The lad had come from Randneck, a suburb of

Sidney. The valiant friend, Chalmers by name, was rewarded for his bravery with a gift of several thousand dollars.

Let all the doubting Thomases go to Manly Beach, where it is necessary to keep constant vigil to protect the swimmers. A large tower stands out in the water over the inlet, where a lookout is on duty all the time. Whenever a shark is sighted entering the bay, a bell is rung to warn the bathers. This precaution saves many lives, but it does not prevent the sharks from taking their annual toll of human beings.

Personal experiences are always the most convincing. One time, by good luck and swift action, we saved our boatman from having his hand bitten off by a shark during manipulations at the boatside. The shark, while still hooked, reached over the side of the boat and grabbed the boatman's hand. Z. G. made immediate use of a club he had laid hold of a minute before and stunned the shark so violently that he released his hold. The boatman's hand was badly lacerated and he was incapacitated for a long time.

Let me repeat—I never did like sharks.

After my second mako fight, we sharpened our stationary gaffs and tied a long line to our detachable gaff. While excitement lagged with me, Z. G. and Captain Mitchell made some splendid catches, of 400 pounds and over. I had not yet hooked a really large one.

Young Romer provided the next thrill for the outfit. He came aboard keen to try out bait fishing with a fly rod. He did, and found it had some of the rush and pep of salmon fishing. But the heavier fish played best on rods with six-ounce tips and nine-thread lines. Romer was busy with such an outfit and had just tired out a large *kahawai*, for which I was reaching with a landing net, when with staggering suddenness the water bulged and out shot a large mako. He grabbed the *kahawai* and shot skyward. He hurled past my face within reaching distance, a black blur that for the briefest moment cut off the light. I was so staggered that I had to take hold of something for support.

"Got him hooked, Uncle Rome!" my nephew shouted. "O boy! Look at him jump!"

I rose to the occasion, grabbed my camera, and tried for pictures. The fish was ten, twenty, thirty feet in the air most of the time. I had never seen such leaps before. He was here, there, everywhere, making me duck and bob to cover him. I caught several snapshots. Unfortunately, my shutter was not fast enough to arrest the motion of that comet-whirling fish. My only results were two fairly clear pictures.

Romer's whole body was alert to his job. His eyes shone with excitement. He played the fish carefully and skillfully, and was sparing with his brawn. His tackle was too light for the fish, and he was wary lest anything break. He put in two tiring hours. Then the mako began to show that the fight was exhausting him, too. Gradually Romer drew him to the boat. He seemed ours as he moved with spent savageness in full sight. But we were too sure. When I reached for him with the gaff, the small hook tore out.

With Romer's misfortune came a break in my luck. Through the days immediately following his experience I caught a number of mako, each time thrilling to the fight and to the power and ferocious majesty of my prey.

It was at the Great Barrier Island, sixty miles from the mainland, that I had my best mako fishing. There had never been any rod fishing around this island; all the fishing was done with hand lines, and only small fish were sought.

[ 169 ]

Market fishermen told impressive tales of repeatedly being cleaned out of hand lines by big makos that appropriated their catches. The great mountain barrier, bold, rugged, impregnable, suggested deep caverns and lurking sea monsters. It was a most suitable haunt for the swift-stalking mako.

By this time it had become habit with me to look for mako fins, as sure a habit as my eternal search for swordfish fins at Catalina. I scanned the ocean early and late. There were times when I forgot I hated sharks. Perhaps unconsciously I had come to think of the mako as another species of fish, had put him in a class of his own. When I watched one jump I had the most thrilling sensations. On sight of a fin in the distance I would hurry toward it, anxious to take on a new battle with a great adversary.

I hooked one off the Needles, a prominent point of Great Barrier Island, and had a high old time with him. I judged him well over 400 pounds; Z. G. figured him 500. I fought him as hard as I would fight a swordfish, and at the end of an hour, during which time I had failed to make any impression on him, the hook tore out.

Several days later I hooked another mako off the same point. I saw him on the surface from a long distance. We ran to him and passed him a bait. I really believe he spied it a hundred feet away. He raced across the water toward it, then sank out of sight, took the bait, and before I could strike commenced to leap. On the first jump he was only fifty feet from the boat. He cleared the water to a height of twenty feet and plunged back. Then almost instantly he appeared again in a clean, powerful leap much higher than the other, and this time described a complete circle.

I gazed in rapt admiration, my rod lying idle in my hand, the line slack. I forgot the camera! I saw my brother's boat racing in our direction, and caught his wild gesticulations and flurry of shouted words, but they meant nothing to me. The mako's stunning display robbed me of thought and action. I have only a priceless memory of those marvelous leaps, no pictures which record them.

The mako did not jump again. I recovered in time to save bungling a fight and settled down to hard work. And it was hard work, more than an hour of it, before I got the upper hand and brought him alongside. I do not mind admitting that I am proud of that catch. He weighed well over 300 pounds—321, to be exact.

Weather conditions were against us at the Great Barrier, and we did not remain long, foremost reason why I was the only one of our party to bring in a deep-sea catch from those waters. Incidentally, I have the honor of being the only person who ever caught a game fish with rod and line off Great Barrier Island.

During the continued bad weather at the Barrier we rescued three men who had been washed ashore in a gale and were cut off from any source of supply by mountain cataracts. My brother sighted their signal fire high up on the mountain and later found their dilapidated boat for them. How closely they escaped being mako fodder! Still, thinking such matters over seriously, if it is written that I am to be devoured by a shark, the indignity will not be so great should it be a mako that is selected to dispose of me.

## CHAPTER XIV

### ON VISIT TO THE LEEWARDS

EVER since Robert Louis Stevenson and subsequent romancers wrote about the South Sea Islands, adventurous souls have yearned to visit the isles of delight; but how very grandiose and sweeping such ambition is can be realized only by its partial fulfillment. The South Sea Islands are too many, too remote from each other on the vast moody sea, some too hopelessly inaccessible, for one man ever to know them all, even were he given several lifetimes to attempt it. And when I say know them I mean stay at each island long enough to remember it as something more than a passing picture.

In 1927 my brother visited Tahiti and several of the atolls of the Tuamotu Archipelago, and the following year planned a return trip on which I accompanied him. Somewhere in those waters live big fish; exactly where was what Z. G. desired to find. His first trip led him to expect excellent fishing in right season, but again—what was the right season? With deep-sea fishing an undiscovered sport there, no one could give definite information.

After several unprofitable weeks at Tahiti we left mid-August for the Leeward Islands of the Society Group. Since the *Fisherman* was limited in its capacity for carrying launches, our two thirty-four-foot boats, which had been freighted south, had to make the trip under their own power. The unbroken stretch of travel on the open sea, through which the launches had to slow to the *Fisherman's* pace, was a hundred miles, and, as previous experience had taught us, wind and storm in that latitude often swoop from the skies without barometric warning, so we knew the trip entailed risk for the boatmen. They, however, were keen for the experience.

Taking into consideration the necessity of entering reef passes in the daytime, which induced us to figure distances at minimum rate of travel, we awaited evening at an anchorage off the west side of Moorea, the majestic island that lifts its cragged walls and spires within sight of Tahiti, and made our start at sunset. It was a peaceful evening with a fair cool breeze, no deceiving calm, but deceiving in its promise.

We were not many hours on the way when the sea ran high, and we clung to the rails of the pitching ship and watched the lights of the launches, with terrifying regularity disappear in the trough of great waves. Squall after squall beset us, at times blotting out the small boats with a black curtain of rain. A deceiving star or two appeared between renewed attacks, but the sea did not flatten a jot. It was a bad night for all of us. Time and again I left corduroyed sheets to go on deck to peer through rain and darkness for the mast lights of the launches.

Early morning brought steadier weather, but sight of nothing but the blue horizon and the white-capped sea. It was nine o'clock before we descried Huahina, the nearest island on our course, and then her spectral silhouette seemed more like a cloud. For the time being we were to pass her far off and head on toward Raiatea, which was acclaimed a good fishing-ground as well as a place of cumulative interest.

What a contrast Raiatea presented to the uniformly over-rich jungle country of Tahiti and Moorea, and again to the flat coral surfaces of the atoll in the Tuamotus. Some of the country was sylvan, some brown as if from drought, and there were great barren lava heights above the jungle woods. The barrier reef was singularly broad, four miles at least, in parts. And what colors! Greens of emerald and aqua marine, azure and orange flames of a fire opal! And bordering on this, and exquisitely distinct, was the traveling white line of breakers and the blue of the restless sea.

Raiatea, a smaller island off Raiatea, and the large island of Tahaa were barricaded from the ocean by a single great length of encircling coral, for in remote ages one great island stood where now thrive its three fragments. Offshore, and within the reef of the main islands, were many islets profuse with coconut groves and bound with glistening white beaches, and, as we presently learned, approachable only in small dugout canoes.

Within sight from Raiatea, but distant and shadowy, reared the strikingly individual outline of the island of Bora Bora, a castle with a round tower, which, Babel-like in height, rose stark and gaunt above surrounding walls.

There are two other islands in the Leeward group, Maupiti and Motuiti, neither of which we visited, though Motuiti, reputed to have most wonderful shoal waters, might well have proved an opulent find for an angler. But with time limited we could visit only Raiatea, Tahaa, Bora Bora and Huahina, and we left even them with a sense of shameful neglect.

The wind was heavy when we came, late afternoon, to the pass at Raiatea. I was sitting on a starboard rail amidships, watching the sailors lower the mainsail with odds against them, when suddenly I saw one of the halyards break and a block and tackle was flung my way. It missed me by less than an inch and fell with a crash at my feet. Had it come higher it would have struck me full force, unless, instinctively, and without thought of sharks, I had taken to the sea. My body was taut for

[ 174 ]

ON VISIT TO THE LEEWARDS

a leap when I realized the deadly missiles would miss me. Z. G. saw this from the poop-deck. "Almost a stranger's face in heaven that time," he said, grimly.

We knew that Raiatea and Tahaa with their many shoals and coral flats were places where quantities of fish would come to feed, but we had not struck the true season for the bait, nor for the big fish which customarily follow the small ones in. The previous year my brother tried out Tahiti and the Tuamotus in June and July, and this second year, on misadvice, we experimented at the Leewards and Tahiti the following months to December. Now, sadder and wiser men, we have figured that the remaining months—late summer and early fall, Tahitian reckoning, must be the time for the coming of big fish, for when we quit in December so my brother could pursue his original plans and go to New Zealand, the bonito were appearing in large numbers and the big fish were slowly tracking them in. I saw one that I hesitate to describe because it was so incredibly large. We did catch some fish at the Leewards; indeed, we had our best sail-fishing there, but we were certain we caught the stragglers of the past season, assuredly not the first-comers of the new.

The day after we arrived at Raiatea, Z. G. and Captain Mitchell each brought in a sailfish; therefore our hopes were extravagant for what we might accomplish in a month. We became popular with the natives and were looked upon as custodians of heaven-sent manna because we turned our catches over to them to dispose of. One or two accidental local catches of sailfish were part history and part myth at the island, so it was great joy to a native to boast that he had actually feasted on one of the creatures.

Two days later I brought in my first sailfish, humbly grateful that I had caught him. Like all fish in the southern waters, he traveled and fought at a speed that out-classed his kin in other localities; he kept on the surface all the time and leaped more than any sailfish I ever played. Here was sport with a thrill.

Prospects seemed bright in the beginning, but actually the fish were scarce. Trusting in better luck, we went to Tahaa for a few days. I have dreamed of a large ship landlocked on a millpond, and I seemed to be reviewing the phenomenon when the *Fisherman* glided for miles through the crystal waters of the reef on the way to Tahaa. During this journey we took to the sea for only a short stretch.

At Tahaa we distributed the steaks of several sailfish among the admiring natives. My bait fisherman, a Tahitian, played butcher with an inimitable gesture of pride.

Every day we fell under the spell of castle-like Bora Bora, and we soon headed her way. On approach the round-tower became a great cylindrical mountain-head which, though it did dominate the entire island, seemed lower and less imposing close at hand. Only distance could give the right proportions. We anchored in a bay at the foot of the mountain. Gray days and frequent showers reminded us of how often from the other islands we had noticed that the high turret was lost in clouds and mist. It seemed to puncture and empty every cloud that came by. The effects of gray shrouds and waterfalls and rainbows were enticing from outside the reef where we passed to and fro in our launches, and we reveled in the beauty of the place, but there were no fish.

A better prospect for fishing was not, however, the only thing that drew us back to Raiatea. We planned to climb its highest mountain in search of a rare flower, to urge the fire-walkers to perform for us, to hold a sailing-canoe race which my brother was to sponsor, and to attend a fish

R. C. GREY WITH FINE MAKO, 321 POUNDS

Z. G. WITH MAKO. NOTE THE LINES OF THIS FISH

drive at Little Raiatea where natives from many islands would foregather.

On our way back to Raiatea, more from habit than hope of raising anything, we rode in advance of the *Fisherman* and trolled as we went. When the launches were in mid-channel, with mine in the lead, I happened to look back and see my brother's boat slowed down and the boatman waving the flag that calls for camera aid, and invariably means a fish in sight.

"Guess it must be a fish," said Thad, in a voice that seemed to supplement—"though I doubt it."

Sid swung the launch round and hooked her up without comment; and I say it takes a pretty consistent streak of bad luck to deaden the enthusiasm of a boatman.

"You bet it's a fish," I shouted, presently.

Not only was the action aboard my brother's boat descriptive of events, but I saw a great black body catapult through the air, then souse into the water again, leaving behind a geyser of spray.

No sooner did I shout, "Marlin!" than out he shot again.

Marlin swordfish it was, and of a size to take my breath and make me half pity and half envy my brother the battle that would ensue. Again and again the fish leaped clear of the water. Sid shut down the engine, and then I could hear Z. G. with acclaiming cries number each jump the Marlin made. "Fourteen! . . . Fifteen! . . . Sixteen! . . ."

A layman, never having seen such a prodigious feat, cannot imagine the power and splendor of it. I have taken on a day's fishing trip friends who have accompanied me more from politeness than from enthusiasm, and through such a sight as a 400-pound fish trying to leap his way to freedom have converted some to the game and given all a topic for conversation that ranks in importance with politics and operations.

But this fish blotted out more sky than a 400-pound fish. I give my word that he ran close to 700.

The *Fisherman* passed us presently and sailed through a reef opening, while we, led off in the opposite direction, were moving out to sea. Z. G. worked fast to recover the line that was spun out by his leaping demon. Forty-one jumps the fish made. For the first two hours he stayed on or near the surface, but after that took to deep water and stubbornly refused to show himself.

The wind was up and the sea rough. The boats rocked perilously. After close escape from being tossed overboard I abandoned my camera stand, took to my chair, and braced myself as best I could. I was half seasick, but I wanted to stay by till the end.

Z. G. toiled desperately. Here was a fish that might save this unpromising trip from being a total loss, here was one of the lesser monsters that he had seen in these mysterious waters, a proof to the claim that he had discovered a third species of Marlin which grows to incredible size. I felt his anxiety, his terrible eagerness.

At three o'clock, after a three-hour fight, the fish sounded 1,200 feet. Always that means the death of the fish and an agonizing finish for the angler, and in rough water the difficulties are multiplied—the fish hangs stationary, and every swell that lifts the boat takes line off the reel. At a time when arms and hands and back ache most mercilessly the angler must use all three with renewed force to lift the beaten fish inch by inch. With the help of the sea this Marlin sank another 200 feet. Z. G. struggled to recover with each pull more than the sea could take out. At four o'clock he had gained all but 150 feet, yet that 150 feet seemed fatefully like a mile.

We were all hanging on hard to the gyrating boats,

The "Fisherman" off Moorea

TROLLING AT BORA-BORA

but scarcely aware of the effort, so intent we were on the painful and gradual intake of the line. Then came tragedy. We saw, but we wanted to discredit our sight. The line, over-strained, had parted. Z. G. with expressive silence wound in the few limp yards that were left. He took the loss of the fish more heroically than I had anticipated, perhaps because those were the early days of our southern visit and he was hopeful for future success, which, sad to relate, did not materialize.

Our return was well timed, for a terrible gale swept the island for the next few days, and Raiatea was our safest anchorage. Even at that, the *Fisherman* dragged her anchors and we were forced to put four cables over, three to shore and one to a sturdy buoy, and the launches had to seek shelter in a small cove down the island.

After the stormy weather abated we devoted a number of days to exploring the island, and photographing, and enjoying native ceremonies. Yet we did manage to break into the program with an afternoon of fishing. Discounting as an excuse the irresistible lure of perfect conditions, we agreed sanctimoniously that we must bring in a fish as a feast gift to the fire-walkers who were to perform for us the following day, and we put out as fast as we could go.

We were trolling a short distance off the reef when I noticed a purple-brown shadow flash behind one of the teasers.

"Sailfish!" I shouted.

Thad had seen him, too, and was at the teasers in no time, while Sid stood by ready to slow down the engines. A mad race usually ensues when teasers are whisked in; somehow the fish will not be distracted from the shiny prize that is being yanked away from him, but follows it close to the boat with a frenzy for capture which he seldom feels for a genuine bait. Outraged at being

[ 179 ]

thwarted by the loss of a teaser, he often refuses to look at anything else that is sent or comes his way. Not so with this one! Though he rushed the teaser, he was ready for the bait. He snatched it greedily. My line spun out as he slithered on top of the water, working up power for a leap.

"There's another," called Thad. "Thought I saw him following."

My fish was in the air, a slim black dart. Quickly he cut into the sea again.

"Captain Mitchell's right behind us," I said, without taking my eyes from the line. "Pass the word to him. He'll get that other beggar."

There was a deal of shouting back and forth, and I heard Captain's boat speeding round. Then we did some speeding on our own account. With movement that seemed all grace and no effort, my sailfish repeatedly reached skyward out of the water. He did not intend to stop. He fled from his enemy and the destruction that threatened him. When he flung the loosened hook off on one of his magnificent propulsions I did not begrudge him his freedom. Yet he was not too sure of his escape. He made four more leaps.

By this time Captain Mitchell was fast to the second fish. Here was another greyhound, swift and tireless.

"But did you get a good look at the size of him!" ejaculated Sid, who had the advantage of a close view while I was working on my sky-flyer.

"Big fellow, eh?" I returned.

"I never saw his beat."

Nor had I, nor had Captain, nor had anyone else in our outfit.

Mitchell played him to the finish, then with the fish aboard rode over to us, smiling.

"Best I ever got," he said.

"Looks like the natives'll get their fish chowder, after all," said Thad.

"Not till I measure and weigh him," Captain assured us.

Later, aboard the *Fisherman*, with everyone from cabin boy to ship's captain looking on, we applied the scales and yardstick. The length of the sailfish was eleven feet eight inches, and he weighed 163 pounds.

That day, while we were fishing, the natives made ready for the fire-walkers' ceremony. They carted stones and a cord of firewood to some cleared land, and then dug a five-foot pit, thirty feet long and twice as wide as its depth. Before sunrise the next morning (the native is consistently an early riser) an enormous fire was started in the pit and fed until it was a bed of red coals covered with flaming logs; then the stones were piled on and other logs were set ablaze on top of the stones. All morning and midday the rocks were heated by roaring fires below and above.

The hour for the ceremony had been set for two o'clock. A crowd of natives came early to the sacred ground, and with them were children who had never before witnessed one of these primitive performances. Seven years had passed since the last one was held.

Apart from the crowd, but within sight, were the fire-walkers themselves, a dozen young men and a dozen young women, and their leader, obviously a priest of importance, who was giving them final instructions.

I was not at all impressed by their costumes; they betrayed the native's pathetic struggle between old teachings and new. Fanciful skirts of long slender leaves, that would have been charming over bright *pareus*, lost all semblance of beauty over modern dresses and long white trousers, and brought to mind a college boy's burlesque of some time-honored custom. Several girls, unwilling to sacrifice the lucious warm color of their *pareus*, wore them draped over their shoulders like shawls, and several men had bound theirs like breech cloths over their trousers. Adjudging the trousers fair compromise, the men wore nothing above their waists except the chains of flowers without which no festive costume is complete. The girls wore necklets, too, and everyone had a floral crown. All were barefoot.

The fire in the pit, and that on top of the rocks, burned as lustily as ever, and steam rose wherever raindrops from slight showers struck the stones. Presently several natives, who had been hovering near the pit, scattered the top fire and cleared away all the logs and cinders. Meanwhile the fire-walkers lined up, girls and boys in pairs, and the priest presented to each performer a sheath of long shiny leaves that reminded me of flax, and reserved one for himself.

Carrying these wands high, like torches, and led by the priest, the young people advanced to the pit in solemn procession. There they halted. The priest beat the stones with his sheath of leaves and muttered incantations to insure safe travel for himself and his followers. Then, smiling and casual, he crossed the pit between tongues of flame that rose from the embers beneath. Close on his heels came the other walkers, but not smiling, and inclined to quicken their steps. They did this repeatedly, going sometimes lengthwise over the stones, sometimes crosswise, and halted between actions to present their wands in different ways, far to the right or far to the left, or straight before them, higher or lower.

Their many walkings achieved, the priest went through prayer and invocation to make the rocks safe for any onlooker who had courage to follow him. Not many ventured at first, and some who did jumped off the sides, but after a few of the volunteers rushed across safely more

THE FIRE-WALKERS

Z. G. with South Sea Marlin Swordfish, 434 Pounds

people took heart to attempt it. However, these laymen were shod. I tested the stones, and I tried the walking, which resolved, as it had for the others, to a hop, skip and jump. No doubt of the scorching power of those stones or the great heat that curled up around you as you hurried over them! I marvel that the natives had not burned their feet unmercifully. A white man could not cross the pit barefoot. The callous of a native's feet must be as heat-proof as leather, for, remember, the tops of the stones were freshly hot when the ceremony started.

To conclude the performance the fire-walkers threw other firewood on the stones, and the new logs ignited in an incredibly short time.

Legend has it that centuries ago the host at a cannibal feast was sorely tried because the carcass of his victim would not cook, although fire had been burning for hours under the rocks he was using as a broiler. Never before had a native oven acted that way. Strange to relate, the anticipated roast had not even scorched, so the banquet had to be called off. The chieftain pondered over this and took up the matter with the high priest. The clergy investigated. The rocks of the oven were new and they were lava. Secretly the clergy agreed that lava rock could reach a heat so great that it lost its power to burn. Here was knowledge they must not permit to escape them, so they advised the chieftain to forget the incident and not discuss it further. Whereupon the priests used this knowledge to prove their powers, instituted the fire-walking ceremony, and convinced their gullible followers that they could pray the rocks into temporary harmlessness.

This story was passed on to me by a white man who had lived most of his life at Raiatea. I did not quite know what to think of his yarn, but finally I accepted it along with the fire-walkers' ceremony as an interesting bit of entertainment.

[ 183 ]

The fact remains that the natives took the performance seriously, were reverent and inspired by faith. I was interested to find that the long leaves carried by the walkers were not affected by the heat of the rocks, which, I observed, were not all lava, and when laid across them did not shrivel like other leaves exposed that way, but retained their freshness and luster, and were not destroyed unless thrown into the flames. These leaves to the native were symbolic of the impotency of the fire when under the spell of the priest.

The heat of the great oven was not wasted. A feast was held in the evening, and sailfish and pork roasted on the stones.

At the end of that week we took to fishing again. I drew two blank days. On the third day, late afternoon, my luck changed. We had about given up and were headed for the *Fisherman* when I saw two dark objects behind my bait, sailfish racing like mad to get to it. One snatched to get it, then quickly released it. The other took a try and behaved the same way.

"What do you know about that?" I said to the boys. "That bonito is too big for them. It's more than they can handle."

The first fish came at the bait again; twice he took it in his mouth and rejected it. Promptly Thad handed over another rod with a mullet on the hook.

One fish swam directly in the center of our wake, but the other had veered to the left of us. The persistent fish came straight for the new bait and smashed it off clean. Forthwith Thad handed me a third rod. The minute I put the line over our gluttonous friend came back, and took the second mullet, hook and all. I yanked it into him hard. He tore off without delay, and soon was lashing the surface in short frantic leaps.

The other fish stayed with us, anxious for a free meal

but unwilling to come close for it. I played the hooked sailfish strenuously, and gobbled up line after the manner of a small boy eating his first piece of pie with a possible second in view. Before I brought the one to gaff, the other decided to leave us. Still, I was happy to make one more catch before we left the Leewards.

He was a beautifully proportioned fish, measuring ten feet four inches.

Had we not arranged to take motion pictures in Papeete of old Tahitian legends, which were to be presented in pantomime, and there to refuel and take on water for a visit to the Tuamotus, we might have prolonged our stay at Raiatea. Then, after our reluctant departure, a frightfully stormy passage to Tahiti developed a situation that, after all, forced us to change our original program. The launches had greater difficulties on the return trip than they had on the way to Raiatea, and one of the boatmen refused to risk the 200-mile run to the Tuamotus, while two were willing but not eager. Thad alone staunchly scoffed at the idea of possible catastrophe. There was no sense in cruising around the atolls without the large launches, because intense fishing was the object of the trip. Z. G. hesitated to ask the men to attempt something that seemed extremely hazardous to three of them, so he called the trip off.

The Leeward cruise was the *Fisherman's* last service for Z. G. Before he left Tahiti for New Zealand he sold her to Father Rougier, a Frenchman of means, who owns Christmas Island. Now my brother dreams of explorations still farther afield, which will call for a larger ship with sufficient space for all launches and great capacity for fuel and water.

Father Rougier has converted the *Fisherman* into a freighting schooner to carry copra from Christmas Island to San Francisco. Thus will she continue her travels up and down the lonely lanes of the Pacific till the end of her days. It saddened me to see her leave our anchorage for Papeete. She rode out the pass sailing the Stars and Stripes for the last time, and gallantly dipped it in a farewell salute.

Her new owner has resumed her maiden name. The *Fisherman* has passed. Long live the *Marshal Foch!*

ℓℓℓℓℓℓℓℓℓℓℓℓℓℓℓℓℓℓℓℓℓℓℓℓℓℓℓℓℓℓℓℓℓℓℓℓℓℓℓℓℓℓℓℓℓℓℓℓℓℓℓℓℓℓℓℓ

CHAPTER XV

## NATIVE FISHING IN THE SOUTH SEA ISLANDS

FISH and the coconut tree are the two essentials of life for natives in the South Sea Islands. While the latter provides shelter as well as food, the former supplies occupation as well as recreation and what is to the native the most delectable supply of his limited daily menu. The islanders enjoy every attainable variety of fish and crustaceans and eat them raw, soused in lime juice, broiled and fried, and, in places where contact with civilization has versed them in culinary arts, prepare with cooked fish sauces worthy of the Plaza grill. In late spring and summer small fish are so plentiful that the cares of life are few, but in off season it takes diligent work to keep the larder supplied.

On my recent trip to Tahiti and the Leeward Islands I observed closely the several native methods of fishing. Everyone is adept at the game, men, women, and children.

Girls wade knee-deep on the reefs in search of small pan fish. Usually they are dressed in scant Mother Hubbards, in lieu of the now seldom-worn *pareu*, and their heavy braided hair hangs from under a large reed hat, and fish bags made of grasses swing forward from their shoulders. They wield bamboo poles, twelve to fifteen feet long, with lines of the same length baited with pieces of shrimp on small hooks. Because the native is naturally gregarious and seeks companionship at work as well as play, it seemed to me solitary women and children anglers must be fishing to meet very present demands.

Boys, more venturesome than their mothers and sisters, cross the deep waters of the reef in their dugout canoes to fish in the white foam of the breakers. Sometimes the women and girls join them. But I think the pure impromptu meal is raised offshore, where I have seen a raw and still wriggling fish being calmly devoured by a dusky-eyed native daughter.

My brother had in his employ a native and his wife who camped near by, and their lives demonstrated that in Tahiti, as elsewhere, "man's work is from sun to sun, but a woman's work is never done." Every evening when their gardening work was over the lord and master would stretch out under a coconut tree to watch the colorful approach of sunset, while madame fished the reef for supper, and then prepared and served the meal. Never once did I see the husband alone on the reef, for when need was immediate fishing held no charm for him. He would, however, go net fishing with some friends if he felt in a holiday mood.

On such occasion the natives set the net in shallow water, making a long triangular trap; then they waded out a good distance, in direct line with the open end of the net, formed a semicircle, and then returned, beating the water and slowly closing in toward each other as they came, in order to scare and chase before them into the net whatever fish happened to be near.

Spear fishing on the reef is popular with the men. The spears they use are twelve feet long and have five or six iron prongs. Stalking the fish as stealthily as a person stalks game, they keep constantly on the alert, and when they see a fish coming their way, they slip up slowly, hurl their spears like javelins, and pin the fish to the coral. They are so accurate in aim, so swift in action, that the fish's chance for life is slight. A hard strike will spread the prongs of a spear, but the native takes care to adjust them whenever it is necessary.

## NATIVE FISHING IN THE SOUTH SEA ISLANDS

There are places in the deep waters of the reef where the coral grows in formation resembling a tree, spreading from a main trunk to many branches and twigs. Some are white, some blue, and others yellow, rose, and lavender. Here each small fish has a kingdom of his own. I have never seen more beautiful palatial aquariums than the colorful abodes supplied by the arbor-like coral. At times the waters of the reef are still as a mill pond, and through them one can see these enchanted palaces, and fish of a thousand colors weaving in and out of the subaqueous passages, their flashing brilliance contrasting with the pastel shades of the sheltering coral. When the water is gently ruffled, with the sun shining through it, the sea floor below appears uniformly laid with rounded tiles of lapis lazuli. These rich places are invaded by the natives when they dive for fish.

I would not care to duck for my dinner as the Polynesian often does, but I must say I do enjoy watching him do it. He carries a single-pointed spear, extra sharp, about the same length as the one he uses when wading, and wears goggles like those used for pearl diving, which make it possible for him to see underwater. Spear in hand, he dives from his canoe or some projection on the reef, with action that frightens the fish into the pockets of the coral. A fish, on being pursued, instead of finding safety there, becomes confounded; then the native with swift eye and motion spears him, and promptly comes up smiling.

Amaru, the native boy who worked aboard my launch, was the first person to introduce me to such fishing. One afternoon, coming in along the reef from a day at sea, he asked me if I would mind letting the boat drift a few minutes—not in those words, to be sure, but with elaborate sign language and one or two English substantives. Curious to see what he was about, I had the engines slowed down. He took up a single-pronged spear, which was part of the paraphernalia he always carried with him, and to my amazement and consternation dove overboard. The water was quiet, and I could see him plainly, but I was not sure at first what he was about. Up he came with a fish wriggling on the end of his spear. Grinning with delight, he clambered aboard. "*Kiki*," he said, which meant food.

He displayed his catch to me. "*Miti*," he said, rubbing his stomach graphically and winking. It was plain that *miti* meant good.

Over he went again. Three times he dove, and each time he came up with a fish. The third time he was very excited. He made no attempt to free his catch from the spear, but brought it still fast for my inspection. "*Itamiti* [no good]," he said.

He pointed gingerly to the dorsal fin, which was sharp as a needle, and again said, "*Itamiti*."

It was a poisonous fish which all native people claim deals a fatal prick with its spiny fin.

Sometimes twenty-five or thirty canoes will engage in fish diving. First the men drive the fish, not depending on the few that frequent the coral pockets. They circle round from inshore and slowly close ranks toward the reef, meanwhile beating the water with their paddles. Arrived at the reef, they await word from their leader, then, altogether, they pile overboard with their spears, and disappear, poles and all, in the deep water.

Their canoes are dugouts, as slender as racing shells, equipped with outriggers. The outrigger is a balancing contraption made of a heavy straight branch of wood which floats parallel to the canoe, two feet away or three, according to the size of the craft, and is made secure there from both stern and bow by slender arched branches. Handled properly, the canoes ride like corks. The native

R. C. at Raiatea with South Pacific Sailfish, New Species

Net Fishing on the Reef, South Seas

has his own safety devices, but he is daring and expert.

Most picturesque of all is the night fishing in the dark of the moon. Then what look like moving fires are abroad on the sea, strange, spectral, and long burning. They are the great torches which the natives make from the dried-out fronds of the coconut tree, and use on moonless nights to startle fish and give light for their capture.

The natives travel with two to each outrigger canoe, one to paddle, the other to play dual rôle of fisherman and torch-bearer. The latter person stands in the bow, torch in one hand, spear in the other, intent on the water over which he glides, ready to throw his spear at sight of a leaping fish or a swift silver gleam beneath the surface, while the boatman is equally alert to follow up the spear as soon as it is thrown. I used to watch these swift silent anglers of the night from the deck of the *Fisherman*, enjoying the beauty of the far-away moving lights, and wishing luck to those spearsmen who came so close to the ship that they were silhouetted against the darkness by the glow of their torches. During the last months at Tahiti, when we lived in camp, in cottages on a high peninsula, I could see the moving fires in two great bays, and at times was waked from sleep by the flickering illumination from a passing canoe.

In October the natives, with more zeal and concentration than I had dreamed them capable of, engaged in canoe repairing for the next and following months when the bonito season would be in full swing and the year's harvest come. The season lasts six months, and is at its height in January.

The bonito come in to feed on schools of *ouma*, a two- or three-inch fish. The bonito, themselves in schools, travel on the surface on track of the bait fish, and over them hover boobies and black gulls and terns. Never have I seen fish and birds travel so fast as those I found in the

South Sea Islands. With both it is part of the fight to survive. Since the water is so clear, the fish are exceedingly
alert, and to avoid their enemies travel with a tremendous precipitation; on the other hand, their enemies,
urged by necessity, double their speed, and life becomes
for all of them a long hard race. There have been times
when my boat, traveling ten knots an hour, could not
keep abreast of the bonito schools, times, indeed, when we
could not overtake them, and I beheld the distant flight
of the anxious birds in hopeless exasperation.

Most of the natives' bonito fishing is done outside the
reef, not far to sea. They use a long stiff bamboo pole,
twelve to fourteen feet in length, with a line about two
feet shorter than the pole. The poles carry two or three
lines. The bait is a two-and-a-half- to four-inch lure made
from pearl shell and cut like a toy canoe. A copper hook is
used the same length as the lure. It fits snugly down the
center of the inside and is bound at either end by fine line
run through small holes bored through the shell. The hook
has no barb. Pig's bristles that look like a small mustache
and simulate a fish's tail are fastened to the hook end of
the lure. The man who lives in affluence has three lines
and three lures permanently attached to his pole. The
lures are always of three different shades—one white, one
gray-white, and a third a golden yellow—because the
practicability of any one of these colors varies with the
conditions of water and weather. The native is prepared
to changes lures whenever it is necessary, and he keeps
the idle ones hooked into a band of fishing line wound
near the butt of the pole.

The lures are neat, pretty, and effective. They ride the
water boatwise, slipping along easily, led with a weaving motion which entices the bonito. The idea of a barb-
less hook is for rapid release of a fish. When a fish bites,
the native snaps him out with a swift fly-casting motion,

landing and freeing and recasting in one continuous action. Occasionally when fish are thick, and he is working fastest, he loses a few overboard, but they are not missed when the haul is two or three hundred. It is no boy's job because the pole is poker stiff and the fish are husky fighters.

At the time when large catches are frequent, the market at Papeete is flooded with bonito and everywhere throughout the outlying districts men go about selling fish from carts, blowing lustily on conch shells to stir up trade.

While we were at Little Raiatea, in the Leeward Islands, we saw one of the justly famous fish drives which are the zenith of all Polynesian fishing. Usually the drives are held only when fish are plentiful, and, since they are occasions of wide social as well as economic importance, at the most, several times a year. Because consent must be obtained from the French administrator before a drive may be held, I am of the opinion that legislation must have been found necessary in former years, when, I understand, fish were far more plentiful and drives held more frequently, so frequently, perhaps, that the fish were frightened to other islands.

Monsieur Capella, the administrator of the Leewards, and his wife accompanied us to Little Raiatea, which is five miles from the large island, the seat of the local government. Our launches could not take us the full way up the reef to our destination; we had to wade half a mile through water or take to thorny jungle, and we found the water not only a simpler but a cooler way of travel.

Little Raiatea has a natural fish trap. Through a converging reef runs a deep narrow channel which takes the shape of a hook and turns inward at the point where the land and reef-edge almost meet, bringing the deep water directly offshore. There the natives have dammed up a pool twenty by forty-five feet, allowing a five-foot inlet; and into this the fish are driven.

The whole performance had a magnitude which I did not anticipate. Five hundred natives met us, men, women, and children, who had come from far and near in their sailing-canoes to hold a drive for the delight of foreign guests. A local princess received us under a canopy of *pareu* coverings, and as is the custom at social gatherings, decorated us with floral wreaths and necklets. The natives in red *pareus*, and garlands as we were, gave gay coloring to the scene.

After our formal reception songs of greeting were sung, followed by prayer led by a Polynesian who seemed to be master of ceremonies, during which, in deference to missionary teaching, floral adornments were removed and naked waists covered by an extra *pareu* or a tattered shirt. Prayer over, the drive was on.

With a fair wind to speed them, thirty men set out in their sailing-canoes to the place from which the fish were customarily driven. It was at the wide part of the reef, a mile down from the fish trap. There they took in their sails and turned about, and lined up as they would for a race, with canoes about fifteen feet apart. Meanwhile some two hundred and fifty men, women, boys, and girls ran down the beach, bearing stout cudgels which were soon to be brought into play, waded out to the channel and lined up on either side, so they described the hooklike curve its water took.

Then all eyes turned to the starting-point. The master of ceremonies, with great aplomb, delivered the anticipated signal by waving a *pareu* mounted on a bamboo pole. At once the canoes advanced, paddling fast and keeping abreast. Their course ran along the reef, just inside the breakers, where the largest number of fish lay.

NATIVE WOMAN FISHING

Start of the Fish Drive

The fish, frightened by the approach of so many boats riding so close, instinctively tried to escape, yet without deserting the friendly coral beds, so while they hurried before the threatening power, they did not attempt to leave the reef-edge, but followed it toward the channel. The closer the land and reef converged, the nearer the boats drew together, and when the fish showed alarm at the strange narrowing of the shoal water and tried to turn back, the men confounded them by beating the water with heavy rock pestles attached to ropes. There was nothing for the fish but the forward flight which led them inevitably to the channel; but to further insure it, the boats changed swiftly to semicircle formation, and cut off escape from all sides.

Once the fish struck the channel, the natives who were lined up there, with shouts of barbaric delight, started threshing the water with their cudgels, so precipitating the flight of the fish that they tore on ahead without regard for their slight chance for freedom in the shoal waters beyond. They sped down the channel and crowded each other through the narrow opening to the pool where they milled round and round, seeking escape. Some natives were on guard at the neck of the pool to keep stragglers from turning back, by disturbing the water and frightening them. Others dragged to the scene a tremendous rope of green palm leaves, as large in girth as the trunk of a coconut tree, and when cries assured them that the last fish had passed, they piled it up in the opening to dam the water of the pool which had become a maelstrom from the frantic movements of the fish. There were several varieties of fish captured, large ones and small ones, and some very striking in color.

That was not all. The master of ceremonies approached my brother with a long four-pronged spear and invited him to take the first fish. It did not seem sporting to spear

[ 195 ]

a trapped fish, but it was up to Z. G. to receive the intended courtesy with appreciation. He strode in among the fish, set eyes on a beauty, and nailed him to the coral. It sounds simple enough, but as I have found since, it was not so simple as it sounds. Even before Z. G. could release the fish, dozens of natives, all bearing spears, rushed in with demoniacal cries of delight. It was a truly savage scene. The way those men, without loss of motion, speared a fish, flung him free on the beach and respeared, reminded me of their bonito fishing, but left me more breathless. Fish and spears flew through the crowded scene, and I wondered that no one was hurt.

Toward the close of the *mêlée*, an absurdly stout native slipped on the coral and pitched head first into the water. The others, with shouts of laughter, quit fishing and piled on the corpulent spearsman, making it impossible for him to rise. Meanwhile boys went barehanded after the remaining small fish, and I saw several betrousered lads walk off with wiggling tails beating above their hip pockets.

There was no communistic division of the fish, and there was no evidence of greed and no dissension. Monsieur Capella explained to us that although some of the fish captured were poisonous and if eaten made one ill, as the natives well knew, nevertheless, because of their savoriness they were happily accepted and would be eaten with the rest. The native enjoys today fearlessly and lets tomorrow and its ills take care of itself.

Throughout that morning I was busy with my motion-picture camera recording the action that I here have attempted to describe. I shall have no end of pleasure reviewing the scenes of the fish drive, but I shall miss the vivid coloring. The flame of red *pareus*, the rainbow effects of the flowers, the green of coconut trees that fringed the gleaming beach, the emerald heights of near-

[ 196 ]

The Fish Trap

THE AUTHOR WITH HIS LARGEST SOUTH SEA MARLIN, 357 POUNDS

by mountains, the remote purple island, cameo-clear, blue horizons and trade-wind clouds like great white ships at anchor, the opalescent waters of the reef, the cobalt sea beyond beating itself to white destruction along the miles of coral wall—these made a symphony of beauty which cannot be translated, but which I shall never forget.

CHAPTER XVI

SEVEN BROADBILLS IN ONE YEAR

RECOLLECTION of my earliest fishing carries back to an adventure I had when I was six years old. My brother refers to it in the Introduction of this book, and wrote of it in his story, "The Fisherman," where I appear as Homer, and he as Lorry, and makes a point of the fact that I started my fishing career with the idea of hanging on. Since I cannot do the occasion justice, let me quote his narrative in brief:

. . . "The minnow pole is up there," said Lorry. "Go to the deep place I showed you—the last one. Catch some and hurry back."

Homer vanished through the green foliage. Whereupon Lorry took up the pole and once more attended to the fascinating watch of that cork. Gradually his excitement subsided. It seemed he was not going to have another bite right off. Something cast a blight upon the marvel of the hour. It oppressed Lorry. At length he discovered the reason—he should not have sent Homer off alone.

Lorry was in a quandary. Here was the wonderful day—precious moments on the creek—and he could not stay longer. Homer was only a little tad. He might fall into the creek or get lost. Lorry reproached himself, and manfully fought the most irresistible temptation to go on fishing. But then for the first time he realized he cared more for Homer than anyone, except their mother, and he could not stay.

Taking pole and bass, he climbed the bank, and set into a run along the shady winding path of bare packed sand. It seemed a long while before he reached the mouth of Joe's Run. Here he slowed down to a walk and followed the edge of the bank.

It was now only a short distance to the place where he had directed Homer to go. Lorry reached it. No sight of Homer! Filled with dismay and a growing concern, Lorry again broke into a run. What would Mother say if anything happened? But Lorry knew

[ 198 ]

he would never go home without his brother. Suddenly he heard a cry. It came from behind a patch of willows.

"I'm comin'," he called, hopefully.

He bounded along, beyond the willows, to a high bank. Like the one below, it slanted to the water. In the middle of it lay Homer, head down, on his stomach. His arms were outstretched and he appeared to be slowly sliding down. His bare toes were digging into the dirt.

"Homer! For the land's sake!" yelled Lorry. "What're you doin' there?"

"Fish! Whad-dye s'pose—you dumb fool—hurry!" panted Homer. Then Lorry made the astounding discovery that Homer was holding to the butt end of the minnow pole, which was half submerged. Something was tugging hard on it. Lorry saw a whirl in the water.

"Hang on!" he yelled, and plunged down, just in the nick of time to save Homer from sliding in. Lorry grasped his brother and hauled him back. "Hang to the pole!"

"I'm—a-hangin'," said Homer, valiantly.

Lorry got him turned round with his feet on a level place. But the fish, whatever it was, appeared too heavy and strong for Homer.

"Gimme the pole!" cried Lorry, almost roughly.

"Aw, he's my fish!" gasped Homer, clinging for dear life to the pole.

"All right, hang on an' I'll help," said Lorry, and suiting action to words he laid hands over Homer's. But this was not to pull hard, for Lorry distrusted the line and hook. It happened, however, that on the way from Joe's Run to Licking Creek he had put a larger hook on the line, intending to let Homer use it for sunfish. This he had forgotten. The remembrance encouraged Lorry in the hope they could catch the fish. So he merely helped Homer hold the pole while the fish swam around until it got tired.

Lorry saw a bright red tail, and then he knew what kind of a fish they had. Presently he got the line in his hand and slipping the fish out on the mud he grasped it and carried it in triumph up the bank. Homer had hung to him like a leech.

"There!" exclaimed Lorry, dropping the prize on the grass. "Big red-horse sucker!"

Homer dropped on his knees in an ecstasy and he babbled in

glee. The fish was a foot and a half long, glistening white all **over** except the tip of his tail, which was red.

"Ooo-ooo!" crooned Homer.

"Say, Bub," queried Lorry, severely, suddenly remembering something, "why didn't you let go that pole?"

"Lorry—I couldn't," replied Homer.

"Why not, I'd like to know," demanded Lorry. "He was pullin' you in."

"I didn't care—I couldn't let go. An' I wouldn't if I could."

That answer silenced Lorry, and in after years he recalled it many times.

Over forty years have passed and I am still hanging on. I have had many exciting and wonderful fishing experiences, but only once in all this time have I been compelled through exhaustion to pass the rod to my brother, and that was in my first encounter with a broadbill, of which I have written in a previous chapter.

I have spent the past eleven years in pursuit of the broadbill swordfish, and I want to go on record as saying that I think the broadbill is the greatest fish that swims. His prodigious strength, endurance, and vitality are undisputed. Speaking from long experience with all the greatest of game fish, and making judgment only after careful comparison in these particulars, I maintain that the broadbill has no peer.

If you lack nerve, endurance, and patience in abundance, keep shy of broadbill fishing, for the broadbill is a wary fish that seldom takes a bait, and when the great occasion does come can give you more hours of vigorous entertainment than any of his finny relatives. Skill at the game comes only with experience, as in any other line of endeavor.

My brother's first broadbill, taken on twenty-four-thread line with piano-wire leader, put up a fight of six hours. Yet he weighed only 260 pounds. During the ensuing years we had many long and thrilling battles, the most notable ones covering periods lasting from five hours to eleven and a half hours. The longest three fights, all of which terminated unsuccessfully for us, ran nine hours, ten hours, and eleven hours.

Other fish of size much greater than any of the broadbill swordfish we have taken failed to show anything approaching the endurance and pugnacity of the broadbill. My largest tuna, 638 pounds, was taken in forty-five minutes. However, to give this fish due credit, I must admit that part of the speed in his capture was attributable to the fact that he was hooked in the throat. Add to this my brother's black Marlin of 704 pounds, which was taken in less than three hours, and his world's-record tuna of 758 pounds taken in three hours and ten minutes. Captain Mitchell was less than three hours bringing in his 976-pound black Marlin. My largest broadbill to date is 588 pounds, and the time was four hours and fifteen minutes. This broadbill is giving 388 pounds to Captain Mitchell's black Marlin, 116 pounds to my brother's black Marlin, and 170 pounds to his record tuna.

Consider the lesser endurance of the broadbill's first cousin, the Marlin swordfish. In capturing my many Marlin the time was usually under two hours; indeed, my largest of this species, 368 pounds, was taken in thirty minutes.

The broadbill's sword is a most formidable weapon. He never hesitates to attack whales and other cetaceans, and after stabbing them repeatedly, generally retires from the combat victorious. No one knows what circumstances excite a swordfish to such attack, but he follows this pugnacious instinct so blindly that he often charges small boats and ships in a similar manner, evidently mistaking them for cetaceans. He pierces the light canoes of the natives of the Pacific Islands with utmost ease, and even heavier boats of the swordfishermen, and often dangerously wounds the individuals who occupy these craft.

Professor Richard Owen, testifying in an English court in regard to the broadbill's violence, said "It strikes with the accumulative force of fifteen double-headed hammers. Its velocity is equal to that of a swivel shot, and it is as dangerous in its effect as a heavy-artillery projectile."

Among the specimens of planking pierced by swordfish, which are preserved in the British Museum, there is one, less than a foot square, which incloses the broken ends of three swords, bespeaking of three fish that concentrated their attack on the same vulnerable point of their supposed enemy.

From personal observation and information gathered it would seem that the broadbill invades all seven seas. Swordfish are pelagic fish, and either singly or in pairs, or in smaller or larger companies, roam over the ocean of the tropical and subtropical zones of both hemispheres. Some species journey regularly into the temperate zones.

As to their spawning-grounds, information is rather vague. The Mediterranean is the one place where the small fish are found in any numbers. Fish eighteen inches in length are reported there. During the months from November to March they are so plentiful that they are marketed as a common article of food.

The swordfish lives on bait fish of local species. He procures his food by piercing and stunning a number with his sword, and gobbling them up one after the other.

Market fishing for swordfish on the Atlantic, in the vicinity of Boston and on the Georgian Banks off Nova Scotia, has been an established business for many years. The broadbills are harpooned and caught in quantities during definite seasons. They are regular in their appearance at these places. On the Georgian Banks they are first seen between the 10th and 20th of June. Then at the approach of cold weather in October they disappear. During the warmest days when the water is calm the broadbills rise to the surface to sun themselves. Many are found asleep. This makes capture of them by harpooning a simple performance.

All broadbill market fishing-boats are specially rigged with a platform or pulpit which extends twenty feet from the bow of the craft. At the end of this pulpit stands a man with a harpoon. The harpoon is attached to six hundred feet of small rope which is tied and bound round a barrel to within a length which gives sufficient play when the harpoon is thrown. As soon as a broadbill is sighted, the fishermen slip the boat his way, till the fellow in the pulpit rides directly over him, in easy range to drive the harpoon home.

Once it strikes into the fish, the harpoon, which is detachable, is released from the pole, the barrel is thrown overboard, and the fish is left to fight or tow the barrel until he becomes exhausted. This obviates any danger for the men and makes them free to immediately search out other broadbill. Often they have several barrels overboard at one time.

Modern market swordfishing is a long cry from the old days when the great gladiators of the sea were harpooned and fought from a rowboat and often themselves took toll in a fair fight.

It is not strange that when harpooned a swordfish should retaliate by attacking his assailant. An old fisherman told me that his boat had been struck many times. One finds on record any number of cases where men were injured and boats laid up for repairs after a desperate encounter. Recently I saw a photograph in a current periodical of a swordfish riveted to the bottom of a boat.

The sword had gone clear through every inch of its length, and the swordfish hung helplessly from the damaged craft, which was being hoisted to the deck of a schooner.

Although the harpooning of swordfish has been going on for many years, there seems to be no depletion of supply. Fishermen agree they are as plentiful as ever, their solitary habits protecting them from wholesale capture.

Rod fishing for swordfish has not been developed to any extent along the Atlantic. The first swordfish ever taken from that prolific area on a rod was captured at Block Island two summers ago.

On the Pacific the facts are the reverse. Rod and line swordfishing has been in vogue for years, but only recently have commercial interests entered and market fishermen attempted to harpoon broadbills. Boats with modern equipment now operate in the waters off San Diego, California.

Broadbills are found in the Pacific all the year round. The great numbers appear in June, July, August, and September, and limited numbers through the other months. Never are they so plentiful as in the Atlantic. But the market fishermen at Redondo, when fishing on the Grouper Banks during the winter months, lose many of their fish to the broadbills, and time and again find one tangled in their nets.

My broadbill swordfishing has been done in the Pacific. I have fished for the broadbill off the coast of southern California, in the waters of Lower California, around the Galapagos Islands, off South America and in New Zealand. Off Magdalena Bay, Lower California, I saw twenty-four swordfish in one day.

Swordfish fight a great deal among themselves. Most of them are battle-scarred. I have counted as many as twenty-six scars on one fish, indisputably wounds inflicted by other swordfish. At times I have found the healing of a recent wound still in progress, and a scar not wholly formed.

I have myself seen swordfish fighting in a school of blackfish. They happened along when the blackfish were attacking a school of porpoise that had fled to our boat for protection and were crowded under it. Some of the porpoise were torn and bleeding, and many were exhausted. The blackfish were too wary to approach the boat close, but they were jumping all around us when a sudden change in antics proved they were themselves pursued. Swordfish leaped among them and rushed back and forth. I could not see any actual thrusts with the sword, but the blackfish were excited to strange gyrations and quit the scene as soon as possible.

During the early years of our broadbill fishing, the twenty-four-thread line and stiff piano-wire leader were used. There were no flukes in catching a broadbill at that time. It was a battle between the angler and the fish, best one to win, and usually, after many hours of Herculean labor, the broadbill won.

Mr. Boschen's fish of 463 pounds, then the record catch, was taken in less than three hours, a very short fight for a broadbill of such size. But upon dissecting the fish it was found that the two hooks (Mr. Boschen at the time was using two hooks) had torn into the heart. It is amazing that the fish was not killed instantly; and the fact that he battled on for almost three hours gives some idea of a broadbill's wonderful vitality.

My brother and I had many doleful experiences while fishing with the twenty-four-thread line. It would be humiliating to admit how many large broadbill escaped because our lines wore out. At times we had fish sounding 500 or 600 feet to die, when our inadequate lines snapped. This experience was common to all the sword-fish anglers, and as frequent. I say it would be humiliating to give figures, because in these days of more sporting endeavor the thirty-nine-thread line does away with the wholesale slaughter of fish, and an angler no longer spends most of his time supplying fodder for sharks.

Recent years have seen the introduction of a new leader. It is of pliable wire, the most destructive and terrible instrument ever invented. It is possible, by slacking line off immediately after one's bait has been taken, to so relieve the tension on this new and exceedingly flexible leader that it will spring into coils and neatly lasso the fish, and in no time, once the fight is on, ingloriously lash and strangle him to death. In the past few years many splendid swordfish have come to this ignoble end. Catches of eighteen, twenty, and twenty-five minutes, and one of six minutes, are recorded. The fish came in welted and lacerated, and there was no denying the method of capture. My brother and I have photographed such catches. I leave it to my readers to judge the ethics of such fishing. To me it is prostituting one of the greatest sports I have ever known.

The summer of 1927 Z. G. remained in the South Sea Islands while I returned to California. This meant that I had to go it alone at Avalon. It was not a pleasant prospect for me. Happy camaraderie had always seemed a part of the pleasure of fishing. I never aspired to be a lone angler. However, I made up my mind to do something worth while. Our launch, the *Gladiator*, had been put in perfect condition, and with the services of Captain Sid Boerstler and Captain Thad Williams, I felt I was able to cope with almost any kind of a situation.

The latter part of June, at the very outset of the season, I ran into very bad weather. Heavy storms had been general throughout the country, and California's good summer weather was delayed. It was cold at Avalon, with heavy fogs, windy days, and rough seas.

On June 27th conditions changed. Morning dawned clear and bright, and although there was still a big swell running—aftermath of days of high wind—prospects were much better.

Thad went to the crow's-nest early that morning. It is rarely we sight any broadbills before ten o'clock, but we were anxious to get started on the long season of work, and everybody wanted to spot some fins. It promised to be quite a race as to who should see the most fish. Thad from his lookout in the crow's-nest had the advantage over Sid and me.

Many net boats were in sight. Thad pointed out schools of albacore, and we noted that the market men were soon on a wild tear after them.

At ten-thirty Sid saw the first broadbill of the season. The fish was away off to the larboard, and might easily have escaped our notice had we been less attentive or less covetous of the honor that fell to Sid. We worked the fish carefully for half an hour. He was shy and diffident. I don't believe he saw the bait at any time, and if he did, he had no desire to look it over.

We ran toward Cape Vincent, off the mainland, until noon. An early westerly wind had come up and the sea was heavy, but on turning back and running with the swell we found conditions more comfortable.

Thad from the crow's-nest, and I from my seat on top of the boat, searched the ocean for the next two hours. We had about given up hope of seeing any more fish that day, when at two o'clock Sid was lucky enough to spot another.

I climbed to the crow's-nest to take the rod while Thad came down to look after the baits. Watching a broadbill's strike from the crow's-nest was a recent idea of my brother's. It beats any other way for thrills. Sitting high above the water you can see the fish's every movement, his approach, his hesitation, his refusal, or his smashing attack.

On the very first pass we gave this broadbill a look at a perfect bait, a fine fresh mackerel that shone brightly in the sun at a seventy-five-foot range. The fish went under with a rush. It was only a moment until he struck the bait a powerful blow.

My legs shook and I was aware of a peculiar sinking sensation which I usually experience when I get a strike from a swordfish. I cannot account for this condition, unless it is subconscious reaction from the terrible physical stress I have suffered in former fights with big ones.

Two blows followed the first strike. Then the fish took the bait and slowly headed away. A moment later I was hooked on. I passed the rod down and hurried to my seat in the cockpit. Such fortune seemed too good to be true —our second swordfish hooked, and everything working well!

Sid arranged gaffs and got my harness while Thad ran the boat. They surely hustled. From their wild prolations I surmised they had the fish hanging on the Avalon pier before he had so much as completed his first run.

I did not command the situation in the first hour. The fish was active and strong and did about as he pleased. No sooner did I decide that it was my turn to dictate maneuvers than without any warning, nor from any great strain on my part, the hook pulled out.

We were all keenly disappointed, but we had had an hour and fifteen minutes of intense excitement, and felt, in view of many past tribulations, that we could call it a day well spent. We went on our way building high hopes for another time.

The weather played pranks the next day, failing in all the promise it had given. A strong east wind blew, and a high surf was running. I had made up my mind to turn back to Avalon because the sea was so heavy and white, when Thad sighted a broadbill. All the time we tried to work him he milled in a circle, making it impossible to place a bait for him. He provoked us in this fashion for a half hour. Sid and Thad said plenty that censors would delete. Sid was for giving up, but Thad and I agreed it was best to try a little longer.

The very first minute that fish took a straight course, he saw the mackerel and came after it in a bee-line. He did not take it at once. He followed it to look it over. Then he struck it a terrific wallop. He must have felt the hook immediately, for he started off like a streak for six hundred or seven hundred feet, gaining momentum all the time. I could not risk letting him go much farther, so while he was traveling at lightning speed I tried to set the hook. He never hesitated on his journey toward freedom. I nearly pitched out of the crow's-nest, but everything held. Sid backed the boat as fast as he could, and meanwhile the fish, at a distance of one thousand feet, sounded. After ten minutes, during which time I tried to recover some of the line, I felt the hook give way.

After much travail in broadbill fishing I have found that any unusual or hurried movements immediately after a strike indicate that the fish has felt the hook. This unusual rush and speed denote fright, and it is only a matter of luck if the fish is really hooked and stays on for any length of time.

On our way home we saw another broadbill. He was wild as a March hare, and we could do nothing with him, although he seemed to look the bait over. It had been a long hard day for us, rolling and tossing around on that rough ocean, but it had afforded us some excitement, and like the previous day was not a total loss.

On Wednesday, June 29th, I hooked a broadbill and fought him for three hours. It was an ideal day and I was working my best, and the boys felt sure the fish was mine by token of its being a third try, and I wanted to believe that with them, though I had learned never to count a fish till he was tied up to the boat. However, we found no magic in this third event. At the very time when the fish was tiring fast, and he seemed most surely ours, the hook pulled loose. It was hard to see that fish go. He looked fully 400 pounds.

To lose three swordfish on three successive days was an entirely new experience to me. I felt it was through no fault of mine, still it was exasperating. The boys were steeped in gloom. There were few comments on the homeward trip.

Avalon boatmen who spend their time fishing for broadbill swordfish become as keen as the angler for success, and are certainly proud of their achievement when a fish is hung before the expectant crowds that gather at the pier.

The fourth day spirits revived and, as enthusiastic as ever, we took up the search. In the morning there were a light fog and a glassy surface on the sea. That indeed is ideal promise for broadbill swordfishing. We found a broadbill at ten o'clock and I was soon hooked on. The Catalina boat, on its way to Avalon, ran right by the *Gladiator*, and gave us a hearty cheer. That cheer would have come in handier at two o'clock when, after a grueling fight, with nothing but a discouraging outlook for the success of the contest, I broke my rod completely off at the tip. At the time the fish was 500 or 600 feet from the boat. I was carrying 1,500 feet of line on my outfit, which gave me plenty to risk making a change of tips. All

SMALLEST OF THE SEVEN

435 POUNDS

hands worked feverishly. We ran the boat in a circle, letting out all the line from the reel to the very last inch. As it spun off toward the end we could no longer feel any strain. This gave happy assurance that plenty of the line floated slack. It was only a moment's work to remove the broken tip and replace it with a new one; then we hurriedly rethreaded the rod and tied the line back on the reel. Once that was done, I reeled in line at top speed, praying for resistance when the slack was removed. All was well. The fish was with us still. He was not, however, ready to surrender. Indeed, he made me doubt such possibility. But after an hour and forty-five minutes of the hardest kind of work he suddenly gave up. I had just enough strength left to bring him the remaining distance to the boat.

This battle, which lasted five hours and forty-five minutes, was fought under perfect conditions. The water had remained fairly smooth all day, and the usual westerly wind did not come up until after three o'clock. It was then too late to do us much damage. Had the wind come up earlier in the day, I am satisfied the fight would have gone against me.

The news that I was hooked to a swordfish had reached Avalon *via* the steamer, and on my return at six o'clock there was a great crowd on the pier awaiting my arrival.

Much to my surprise, the broadbill weighed only 374 pounds.

A swordfish catch so early in the season was surprising luck. We were all elated. Sid and Thad in solemn conference predicted a wonderful season for me.

"Let's celebrate the Fourth of July by bringing in a buster," Thad suggested.

I smiled at his artlessness. He might have been saying, "Let's boost a goldfish out of the aquarium for the Fourth."

It happened that July's first bow was a chilling one. There were a high fog in the early morning and a northeast wind. We saw one broadbill. He came up looking for sunshine, found it too cool and rough, and dove back without wasting much time. Conditions grew worse, so we turned toward the island and made home by four o'clock, tired from buffeting the sea.

On Saturday, July 2nd, Avalon was athrong with a holiday crowd. I laid aside the temptation to be a part of the leisurely mob, for a smooth sea was calling and moderately warm sunshine smiled from clear skies. We ran straight out from Avalon for ten miles. By that time the sun was hot and the ocean a crystal floor. To our practiced eyes a fin showed up like a sail, on such a sea as that. I took to the crow's-nest myself. In short order I sighted a fish, way off to the horizon. I lost him, then picked him up again.

I rushed down to my rod while we shot full power ahead. The fish pepped up as we slowed down to circle him. He jumped clear of the water, and we looked on in a daze of delight. I had little hope of getting a strike after the jump. It seldom happens that one does. He was such a difficult fish to keep sight of, because he played just under the water most of the time instead of surfacing. We had to watch closely to catch the shadowy color of him.

Our first presentation of a bait was not a good one, but he caught sight of it in spite of the fact that we had swung out so far that we put his vision to a hundred-foot test. He rushed it, plowing up the water as he came, and before I had time to think he struck it a terrific blow and promptly started away. I was afraid he had felt the hook, so after letting him run for 600 feet I came up on him with all my strength. The next moment I sang inwardly. He was hooked!

The fight developed into a fast running one. For most of two hours we could see him threshing back and forth on the surface.

"What's the matter with that bird?" inquired Sid.

"Guess he's a fancy dancer," Thad replied, frowningly.

I had had my misgivings. This surface racing was too prolonged to be natural. Moreover, there was a peculiar jerking motion on the line which made me suspect the leader played an unwarranted part in the fight. In a little over two hours the fish came to the boat broadside. The hook was firm in his tail and the leader was bound through his mouth, coming out the other side. This made the strain on the fish severe, and it cut down the time of the fight. It gave a slight illustration of what the new airplane leader could do when tangled round a swordfish. Had this broadbill been firmly lassoed I would have met with one of the ten-minute miracles, and in such case I would have brought him in only as a specimen for photographs and to hand over to the Avalon fish market after our usual custom.

"I said we'd show them something for the Fourth," Thad bragged, happily.

" 'Tain't the Fourth yet," grinned Sid.

"Wal, it'll swing for the holiday crowd," Thad protested. "And maybe we'll show 'em another one by Monday."

"You can't tell nothin' about it," Sid acquiesced.

I laughed.

Up to this time we had sighted seven swordfish, hooked five of them, lost three and caught two, results more remarkable than any I had had in all my years of broadbill fishing. No wonder the boys had such extravagant hopes!

There was no celebration for us on the Fourth of July. The stretch of days from July 3rd to July 12th was most

[ 213 ]

discouraging. We had a northwesterly for three days, and angry white-capped seas—then a mighty ground swell followed by more wind, days when the boat rode drunkenly and there was a scarcity of fish.

On July 8th, the most passable day of the lot, but none too good at that, we saw five swordfish and had one strike, which I missed. At any rate, I had a thrill, the first in a long time. From my position I could see every movement of the fish—watched him circle and recircle—come, look at the bait, refuse it, come again, strike at the bait without taking it, continue in his circle, then return to strike the bait again. He stayed behind it and made a third and a fourth strike. It was wonderful to watch this enormous fish toy with a bait like a cat with a mouse. Satisfied at last that he had killed it, he opened his mouth, took hold of it, and gradually sank out of sight. The minute he disappeared I felt the line slack. For reasons of his own, he decided the bait was undesirable and let go. We pulled it in and found it badly smashed.

Sharks worked the channel hungrily during this period. There were no small fish, nor any birds.

We had an adventure a little later which made up for the misery of all those days. After many dull hours on one occasion of seemingly fruitless quest, I was attracted by a great splashing in the distance, and even before I exclaimed about it I saw a whale in the air. I thought he was jumping for fun, and would continue his frolic, so I called to the boys to run that way quickly and give me a chance to photograph.

At brief intervals the whale showed on the surface, threshing the water violently. That was a new antic to me. I wondered about it. It was too unusual for play. Moreover, he was racing in headlong flight, despite the many times he slacked up for these frenzied movements. We ourselves were running ten knots an hour, and still

452 POUNDS

WEIGHING IN A BROADBILL AT AVALON

we gained nothing on him. The half-turn and the side-long threshing of the tail of the whale indicated some action of defense. I had seen whales lob-tail. It is a violent threshing usually resorted to just before a whale sounds. At any other time it is an indication of fury. This was another order of lob-tailing. The whale shot over the surface with each action, beating air and water, and throwing a tremendous cloud of spray everywhere. It was while I was watching this unusual propulsion that a big broadbill burst out of the water directly behind the whale. Whale and swordfish disappeared together, soon to come on the surface again. Then I remembered the claim of old whalers that a swordfish will attack a whale. If ever it happened it was happening now. The broadbill was following the whale, and at times they raced on the surface almost side by side. We could not keep up with them and were losing distance all the time, but I watched until they disappeared. I am fully convinced that each time the whale's pace was slackened and he floundered so grotesquely the swordfish was piercing him with his sword.

After nine relentlessly fatiguing days we prayed for change. Besides being keen for a fight, we were hungry for another broadbill steak. The meat of the broadbill swordfish is the finest fish food in the world; news that a broadbill has been brought in always sends Avalon housewives rushing to the fish market, and it is a matter of only an hour or two before orders are placed that cover the very last pound.

A cold northeast wind and rough water greeted us on July 12th. It seemed the weather never would be fine again. We ran northeast for a couple of hours and then turned up the channel. There we encountered a heavy swell.

If the *Gladiator* had not been a big, well-designed

[215]

launch with plenty of power, we could not have worked
through so many days of rough sea and wind. There was
no use in running against such a swell, so we turned back
down the channel. At noon the wind changed to southeast, the sun came out, the sea flattened. We looked for
a millennium! When a broadbill fin hove in view a day
of great happiness indeed seemed imminent. He was a
hungry fish. He was anxious lest the bait escape him; he
let us come close, then shortened the distance between
us of his own accord. I have always maintained when a
broadbill wants a bait, neither the approach of a boat nor
any action on board will turn him away.

Surely nothing had terror for our newcomer. In most
welcome manner action speeded up from the very minute
we caught sight of his fin. I was hooked on to him almost
before I was aware of it. He kept me busy for the first
hour and we did considerable running to keep up with
him. I think he wore himself out, for he tired quickly
from that time on and fought deep down with slow determined action, struggling to go down and ever down.
I was two hours and forty minutes bringing him to gaff.
He was a beautiful symmetrical specimen, and turned
out to be the largest broadbill I had ever taken, weighing
435 pounds. It exceeded by thirty-five pounds my fish of
1923, which to this date had been my largest one.

Sid and Thad now claimed we were sitting on top of
the world. The season was far from over and there were
more fish to conquer.

I had been keeping in touch by radio with my brother,
who was pioneering the fishing around the Paumotu
Archipelago. Every time I caught a fish I sped a message
southward. Reports from him were not so encouraging.
He had been meeting all manner of difficulties and was
particularly unfortunate in having the *Fisherman* strike
a reef at one of the atolls. It developed that little damage

was done the ship, though for hours it was feared that the cables upon which hope of rescue depended might give way.

No amount of strenuous labor could make me quail. I was in splendid condition after fighting fish through an eight months' season, which included my New Zealand fishing. What made me marvel was the gracious good fortune of locating the fish when I was most fit to take on all comers. Not that the ocean teemed with them or the weather was over-kind!

We were in for another fruitless period—nine days this time, during which we felt that all the broadbills had disappeared. Part of the time the wind was unfavorable, but even the few good days yielded no sight of a fin.

News had reached us that week about broadbill market-fishing operations off San Diego, the very first word we had of such formidable encroachment on the west coast. The boys were quick to jump at conclusions, and immediately attributed the scarcity of fish to the ravages of market fishermen. I did not agree with them. It was too early an experiment, on too slight a scale, to have such effect.

Following a severe northwester, which lasted for three days, making it impossible for us to fish, the morning of July 17th brought the return of good weather. The fog lifted and bright sunshine and smooth water were with us again. We ran across the channel to the mainland off Balboa. There a slight breeze ruffled the sea. I sat atop the *Gladiator*, basking in the sunlight. The ocean was astir with life. Birds were flying everywhere. Albacore were breaking water all around us and occasionally a big tuna would jump, throwing geysers of white spray.

Presently we saw some whales blowing, and I suggested we follow them for photographs. Sid was never enthusiastic about chasing whales. Years ago, before my

ADVENTURES OF A DEEP-SEA ANGLER

brother employed him, he accidentally ran his boat, the *Katharine J.*, on top of one, and sustained a shock that abides with him still. There is no denying the danger of riding too close to them, but good judgment seems to vanish when you have a camera in your hand and a prospect that holds promise of the opportunity of a lifetime.

We ran up on the whales and found them surfacing. At first they ignored us, seeming not to care that we rode alongside. I kept my camera clicking. Presently they grew companionable, nay, playful, and started diving under the boat and coming up the other side. They moved rapidly, propelling their enormous bodies with an ease that came close to gracefulness. Fascinating as it was, I began to feel uncomfortable. Sid was in misery. I figured it was time for us to retire from the scene, and told Sid to run off from them. The whales, however, would have none of that. They were fond of their new playfellow and meant to keep pace with him. Although we ran full speed ahead, they followed right along with the boat, two playing off the side, and one directly under us. The one under us had me growing goose-flesh. I knew if he took a notion to sound from that position it would be all day with us. The two that flanked us were incredibly swift in their movements, and were bearing toward us all the while. One lob-tailed near us, and that was like the first shot of enemy fire.

We had to devise some way of escape. I was about to suggest that we stop the boat while they pushed on, and see what effect that had, when the two sidling whales began to butt the boat, scraping their sides along the hull. These may have been harmless playful tactics, but they took all the sap out of me. I lost no time articulating. I shouted to Sid to stop the boat and give them all the sea they wanted. As we slowed to a stop they lost interest. I guess they were confident that whatever the game was we were playing, they were the ones who had won. In short order they sank out of sight.

We were a badly disorganized group. I reached for a chair, weak in the knees and wringing wet all over. After this hazardous flirtation we voted unanimously to stay away from whales for a while.

On the morning of July 21st, a few miles offshore from Balboa, I hooked another broadbill. I hooked on at eleven-fifteen and at three-five in the afternoon, in a sea that was running high, I landed him. Our trip back to Avalon was so rough that at times the water shot clear over the top of the *Gladiator*. We did not reach Avalon until six-thirty, then a very tired crew, but our spirits soared skyward when we found that our fish weighed 452 pounds. It was the season's largest broadbill to date.

I was the only one out from Avalon at this time who was earnestly fishing for swordfish. The scarcity of tuna had dampened the ardor of the tuna fishermen, and they did not seem to care to take up the daily grind that is necessary to get results from broadbill fishing.

On July 25th, I caught another broadbill, this one 281 pounds, and on July 27th another one, 392 pounds. Frankly, I was delighted with my success. I felt it was due me—that I had earned it through many years of hard work.

The fish I took on July 27th was number six for me, and gave me a tie with Mr. Boschen's record of six broadbills in a season, which he had established in 1913 and which had not been broken through the years. In my wildest flights of imagination I had never dreamed of matching Mr. Boschen's achievement. Thad and Sid almost strutted when they walked. Were we going to catch another broadbill? Of course we were! Strange to relate, I was as confident as they.

July 28th came. I write this with pagan reverence.

It is a date that will always be a notable anniversary in my family.

The day began with cloud and low fog in the east. We ran along the island toward Long Point and then headed northwest until the island disappeared. We could not see the mainland for the fog. There was a heavy swell, but the sea was strangely glassy. It was cool, working toward the west, so about ten o'clock we turned the boat and worked toward the island again. Soon the sun shone, the wind weakened, and the air grew softly warm.

Thad was in the crow's-nest, and I was sitting on top in the chair. At eleven o'clock I sighted a broadbill. I called out to the boys. Thad, who was studying the sea with me, looked down to say he had been watching these same fins for some time but was not convinced it was a broadbill.

"I'll show you what it is!" I yelled.

Thad hustled below to prepare a bait and I climbed to the crow's-nest and took the rod. I kept my eyes glued to the far-away fins. A broadbill it was! We rode to within wise distance of him and passed the bait perfectly. There was a tense second; then to our dismay he turned off quickly. Sid was sure when a fish refused a bait that way he had a full stomach. I laughed at that and suggested we tempt him with a barracuda. We had one, a fine fresh firm bait.

We circled again. The broadbill saw the barracuda as it passed and made a dash for it. Meanwhile I had Sid keep the boat going to make the bait appear lively. With the light favorable I could see every move the fish made. He came in behind the bait and followed it. Suddenly he made a fierce strike at it, missed it, and turned completely over, showing the white of his stomach. He came back again, welted the bait an awful blow, struck it twice more, then took it and started away. After a run of 500 feet he slowed down. I struck at him several times, then lowered the rod to Thad and went down.

In the next few minutes we created enough bustle and stir for ten men—shouts, commands, ejaculations of joy —rushing to the cockpit, filling it for all its space, and getting hopelessly in each other's way.

The fish gave an amazing exhibition of speed. We raced over the ocean after him. He would turn, come back to the boat, and flash under it like a streak. Time and again he did it. Too often, in fact. It was possible for him to damage the propeller. On this maneuver I put the rod down in the water as far as I could. No other fish had ever driven me to do it so many times. Then he would rant around the boat, tail and dorsal fin out, as if he were working up energy for the long run that would follow. He continued this until we were distracted. A westerly wind rose and the sea grew rough. After two hours the fish slowed down a little and started a dogged fight. Several boats passed us, one the *Black Swan*, which I had last seen when I was hooked on to a big tuna off the coast of Cape San Lucas, Lower California.

At this stage of the fight the broadbill resorted to a new stunt. He would run straight away from the boat for 500 or 600 feet, then come to the surface and stay there awhile. Pulling him to us was impossible, so to regain line we had to run toward him. He would keep his position, idling on the surface, making the best of his chance to rest until we were within a hundred feet of him, ther he would shake his old tail, churn up the water, and start off again. He kept up these tactics for the next hour. Run and rest, run and rest. We ran, but did not get the rest.

I was well worn at the end of three hours, but I was willing to keep on till I collapsed, if necessary. I had had many clear glimpses of this broadbill and knew what a beauty he was for size and shape, and I would not have surrendered to him to spare myself, no matter what it cost. The boys declared he was the grandest and greatest broadbill we had ever seen. I knew he was the largest I had ever met.

More time dragged by—minutes of acute agony for me. I began to have misgivings. No matter how hard I fought, still I could lose this fish. He might throw the hook—he might break the line, revert to his early tactics and cut it on the propeller. I tried to turn from such thoughts.

I had fought without rest for three and a half hours. I was nervous. My knees began to shake. My back and arms seemed clamped in steel which I was forced to lift with each movement. I kept on. Presently there was the slightest release. The broadbill was having his hard time. Bit by bit he slowed up. Each new effort to regain his freedom was weaker. He began to sink slowly, working his head down. Lower and lower he went. My spirits sank with him. If he was going to die at a great depth, how could I, in such state of exhaustion, ever lift him to the surface?

Slower and slower, deeper and deeper, he went. I exerted tremendous strain on the rod, almost heart-bursting. I stopped him. That was a moment of crisis.

But how could I lift him? I went at it doggedly. I ordered the boys to run the boat a short distance off to give a slight leverage; then I started the fish from the bottom. It was true. He was coming!

I went at this, the most difficult task I had ever undertaken, with hope renewed.

At first it was a foot at a time. Gradually the length of line recovered at each pump grew more. Then, after what seemed interminable hours, I felt the line come easier. The nearer I drew the fish to the surface, the less

Z. G. with World-record Broadbill, 582 Pounds

R. C. with World-record Broadbill, 588 Pounds

the resistance grew, and the last few minutes the excruciating agony I suffered seemed also to be passing.

Sid stood by with a gaff; Thad was ready with a rope to bind the fish to the boat. A few more pulls and I had him alongside. Sid reached over with a gaff; Thad slipped the rope over his tail. I seemed to be dreaming this. I almost collapsed.

Joyous exclamations from the boys revived me somewhat. Weak and trembling as I was, I ventured from my chair to look over the side of the boat and view my prize. I was bewildered with delight. I was not much help in loading the fish, but if staring were drawing power, I would have taken all the credit for hoisting it aboard.

On our way back to Avalon we passed time guessing the weight of the fish. I settled on 550, Sid on 575, and Thad on 600.

It was dark when we reached Avalon. Whenever the *Gladiator* fails to arrive before sunset, local people anticipate a breakdown at sea or some unusual fishing adventure, so it happened a crowd of several thousand gathered at the pier to greet us. It took six men to carry the fish to the scales. We had difficulty in weighing him, for word buzzed through the crowd that here was a record, and everyone was so intent on getting a glimpse of the fish that they gave us no elbow room.

It had not occurred to me that I might have a record broadbill. At no time did I think that my fish would outsize my brother's world-record catch of the previous year, which weighed 582 pounds; yet whispers reached my ears to the contrary, and I admit I watched the weighing with conflicting emotions. Presently the man officiating bellowed forth, "FIVE HUNDRED AND EIGHTY-EIGHT POUNDS!" I felt the need of some place to sit down.

My 1927 season started June 25th and closed on September 1st, a total of sixty-seven days. In all I ran 3,450 miles, making a daily average of fifty miles. I saw seventy-nine broadbill swordfish, had twelve strikes and caught seven fish.

The weights and time on these fish are as follows:

347 lbs............ 5 hrs. 45 min.
355 lbs............ 2 hrs. 10 min.
435 lbs............ 2 hrs. 40 min.
452 lbs............ 3 hrs. 50 min.
281 lbs............ 3 hrs. 30 min.
392 lbs............ 2 hrs. 7 min.
588 lbs............ 4 hrs. 15 min.
Average weight, 407 lbs.

I know of ten broadbills that were broken off during this season by Catalina anglers who were using twenty-four-thread lines, and up until September 1st, when I closed my season, only one broadbill swordfish had been taken besides those I had brought in myself.

**THE END**